Barbara March '94.

English Grammar Lessons

Michael Dean

Upper-Intermediate
With answers

Oxford University Press 1993

Oxford University Press
Walton Street, Oxford OX2 6DP

Oxford New York Toronto Madrid
Delhi Bombay Calcutta Madras Karachi
Kuala Lumpur Singapore Hong Kong
Tokyo Nairobi Dar es Salaam Cape Town
Melbourne Auckland

and associated companies in
Berlin Ibadan

OXFORD and OXFORD ENGLISH
are trade marks of Oxford University Press.

ISBN 0 19 431358 1 (with answers)
ISBN 0 19 431359 X (without answers)

Illustrated by Robina Green,
Nick Hardcastle and Martin Cottham
Typeset in Adobe Garamond by
Wyvern Typesetting Ltd, Bristol

Printed in Hong Kong

This book is for my family. For Judith, Leah and for my parents.

Contents

Grammar topic table (contents listed by grammar theme)

Introduction

Using this book

English Grammar Lessons revises and extends the grammatical knowledge of upper-intermediate and good mid-intermediate learners. The book is suitable for classes preparing for the Cambridge First Certificate examination.

English Grammar Lessons can be used in three main ways:

1 The thirty-two units can be worked through in the order they are presented in the Contents and used as a grammar course.

2 They can be integrated with skills work, again following the sequence suggested in the Contents, to form a grammatically-focused general course.

3 The units can also be used selectively and in any order, as they are independent of each other. They can be employed to teach or revise any specific area of grammar that learners are having difficulty with in their oral or written work. To facilitate this selective use, the units are listed by 'grammar theme' in a Grammar topic table. A teacher wishing to teach or revise a theme such as tenses or modal verbs can use any or all of the group of units which deal with that theme.

The structure of each unit

Each unit is made up of four parts, each one page long.

A The starting activities

The starting activities are short activities which introduce the grammar topic of the unit. In these starting activities learners talk briefly in pairs (or as a class), using or discussing individual elements of the grammar topic. This prepares learners for the explanations of when and how to use the grammar which come in the 'Grammar guide'.

B The grammar guide

The grammar guide contains a summary of all the grammar that the learners need for that unit. It is for them to read individually, in groups, or together as a class, after they have done the starting activities. Alternatively, teachers may sometimes wish to ask learners to read the grammar guide at home or in class, before they do the starting activities (if the grammar topic is a particularly difficult one for the class for example). It is also possible for the relevant part of the grammar guide only to be referred to before or after the learners do each starting activity.

C The activities

The activities require the learners to use the grammar from the grammar guide in different kinds of interaction. Some of the activities set up situations where the grammar is used communicatively. Other activities are games, or collaborative tasks, in which learners manipulate the grammar. A third type of activity uses stories or the lives of well-known people as a framework to put the grammar of the unit into a context. The 'Activity notes' at the back of the book (shown by a coloured panel) provide material for the information gap activities and for some of the other activities. The learners do many of the activities in pairs. There are plenty of opportunities for groupwork in the activities, but an alternative way of doing the activity in pairs is always given in case time, or class size, or other factors make groupwork difficult.

Many activities end with classwork (with the rubric 'Work as a class'). Here the whole class can listen to some of the work that was done in pairs or groups. Learners can note down examples of the grammar that other people in the class have used in communication. In this way learners can produce their own organized grammar notes. These notes are particularly useful before examinations.

D Accuracy practice

The accuracy practice exercises are simple written exercises which check that the grammar in the grammar guide to the unit has been learned. The accuracy practice exercises can be set for homework, or done in class. The answers to the accuracy practice exercises are at the back of the book.

1

Present progressive and present simple (present time)

A Starting activities

1 Young people are getting nicer

Present progressive for changing and developing situations

Work in pairs. Imagine that you and your partner are both eighty. Talk to each other about young people today. Use the present progressive to talk about the way young people are changing. Example: *Young people are getting more interested in the environment.*

Ideas: clothes (*wear casual clothes more/less often*); food (*eat more/less meat*); behaviour (*be more/less polite*); money (*spend more/less on . . .*); school (*be more/less interested in . . .*); way of life (*spend more/less time . . .*); interests (*be more/less interested in . . .*)

2 She's living here at the moment

Present progressive for temporary situations

Work in pairs. You both have a guest staying with you for three weeks. Talk about your guest's life with you. Use the present progressive. Each sentence should end with *while she's here*, like this: *She's using my bicycle while she's here.* Use the pictures to give you ideas but try to add ideas of your own.

3 Wrong!

Emphatic *do/does* (present simple)

Work in pairs, A and B. Your partner will tell you some facts that are wrong. Correct your partner when you hear a wrong fact.
Example: A: *Paul McCartney likes beef.*
B: *No, he doesn't like beef. He's a vegetarian.*

Read your Activity note before you start.
Person A: Read Activity note 1 on page 136.
Person B: Read Activity note 42 on page 148.

4 Which is used when?

Present progressive and present simple

Work as a class. Match the sentences (1–6) with the uses of the present progressive and present simple (a–f). For example, the answer to 1 is (e).

1 I live in Paris.
2 She's staying with her aunt at the moment.
3 Love hurts.
4 Her English is getting better all the time.
5 I usually catch the nine o'clock bus to work.
6 Look, that man is stealing a packet of sugar.

Present progressive:
a Action still happening
b Changing or developing situation
c Temporary situation

Present simple:
d Law of nature
e Permanent situation
f Regular repeated action

When you have finished look at Activity note 5 on page 137.

B Grammar guide

1 Present progressive

We use the present PROGRESSive when we talk about an action or situation in PROGRESS. The action is still happening or the situation is still changing.
Use the present progressive to talk about:

- actions happening now or over a period of time around now:
  Hattie is working at the computer at the moment. (now)
  He's reading a book about Japan at school. (over a period of time)
- changing and developing situations:
  It's getting colder. *Black skirts are becoming fashionable again.*
- temporary situations:
  I'm staying with Mark for three weeks.

2 Present simple

The present simple is used when the speaker thinks of something as a fact.
Use the present simple to talk about:

- a law of nature:
  Light travels through space at a speed of 299, 792 km per second.
- a permanent situation, or a state with no definite start and finish time but true now:
  I live in Oxford. *I like fish.*
- a regular repeated action or something on a timetable:
  I play football twice a week.
  The London train leaves at seven o'clock every day.
- a fact that you want to emphasize (emphatic *do/does*):
  Adam: *They never go on holiday.*
  Brenda: *Yes, they* **do** *go on holiday.*
  (Here Brenda wants to emphasize a fact because Adam has said something wrong.)
  We can also emphasize what we see as a fact by stressing *is/isn't* or *are/aren't.*
  Yes, he **is** *polite to people.*

3 State verbs and the present simple

- State verbs are usually in the present simple, because the speaker is thinking of a fact and not of an action in progress.
  The vegetables taste fine. (NOT ~~*are tasting*~~)
  In this example, what is important to the speaker is his or her opinion of the vegetables, not the progress of the action (tasting).
- Some of the most important state verbs are: *see, hear, look, feel, taste, smell, be, seem, want, prefer, believe, hate, know, like, love, realize, remember, suppose.*
- Some state verbs (*see, hear, feel, taste* and *smell*) are often used after *can.*
  I can hear something outside.

4 Present progressive and present simple in context

When we have made it clear by using the present progressive that the action or situation is in progress, we can use the present simple to describe facts about the same action or situation.
I'm reading a book about the 1960s. It gives a clear description of life then and paints a picture of . . .

C Activities

1 Windows

Present simple with state verbs; present progressive

1 Work as a class. Imagine that you are looking out of the window and you can see what is in the picture below. Describe the man in the picture using *I can see* and *He looks* or *He seems.* Then make three or four present progressive sentences about what is happening as you watch from the window. Example: *I can see a tall man. He looks like a . . .. He seems nervous. He is taking . . . from his pocket. Now he is . . .*

2 Work in pairs, A and B. Imagine that you are looking out of the window and you see what is in the pictures on the Activity notes pages. Describe the people using state verbs (*He looks, He seems*) then tell your partner what is happening using the present progressive. Do not let your partner see the pictures. Remember what your partner says about her/his pictures.
Person A: Read Activity note 4 on page 137.
Person B: Read Activity note 70 on page 160.

3 Work as a class. Do not look at the pictures again until you have finished. The people who were B in 2 help each other to describe A's pictures. One of the Bs can draw A's pictures from the descriptions. The people who were A in 2 help each other to describe B's pictures. One of the As can draw B's pictures from the descriptions.

2 Sack Mr Smith?

Present simple and emphatic *do/does*

1 Work in pairs, A and B. Mr Smith is a salesman in the firm you both work for. He sells groceries and vegetables to supermarkets but his work is not very good. In the Activity notes you each have information from a report on Mr Smith's work. Discuss your report with your partner and decide whether to sack Mr Smith. Use some emphatic *do/does* sentences, where you can. Example: *He* ***does*** *have a lot of supermarkets to visit.*
Person A: Read Activity note 2 on page 136.
Person B: Read Activity note 43 on page 149.

2 Work as a class. List the emphatic *do/does* sentences you used.

3 Personal profile questionnaires

Present progressive and present simple

1 Work as a class. You are going to find out as much as you can about other people in the class by writing questions for a personal profile questionnaire. Choose five headings and think of one question for each of them using the present progressive or present simple. Here are some ideas for headings:
Likes and loves (*Do you like spicy food?*); Optimist or pessimist? (*Do you usually do better in tests than you expect to?*); Perfect partner; Ideal evening out; Favourite people; Happy or unhappy?; Favourite books, magazines and television programmes; Hates; Do you agree that . . .? (*Do you agree that young people are getting nicer?*)

2 In pairs, write more present simple and present progressive questions under each heading you have chosen, to make a personal profile questionnaire.

3 Change partners and ask your new partner the questions from your personal profile questionnaire.

D Accuracy practice

1 Complete the sentences using the verbs in brackets in the present progressive or present simple.

1 Please be quiet. I ____ (try) to read the paper.
2 This is a very quiet town. Where ____ (people/go) in the evenings?
3 I ____ (work) in a factory until I can find a better job.
4 What ____ (you/do) with all that paper and glue?
5 I ____ (not/use) the computer at the moment so you can use it.
6 ____ (Karen and John/ever/write) to you?

2 Choose state verbs from the list to complete the sentences. Use each verb once.

smell, hate, know, like, remember

1 She always ____ my birthday.
2 Those flowers ____ nice. What are they?
3 Jane is repairing the car. She ____ how to do it.
4 I ____ (not) him, I just ____ (not) him very much at the moment.
5 ____ you ____ how to say this in French?

3 Reply with sentences using emphatic *do/does* or *is/isn't*.

Example: A: Mr Smith never keeps appointments. B: Yes, *he **does** keep appointments.*

1 A: It doesn't rain here in the summer. B: Yes, ____________
2 A: They never get up before eleven o'clock. B: Yes, ____________
3 A: He lives near Helen. B: No, ____________
4 A: It's over there. B: No, ____________
5 A: He isn't the right person for the job. B: Yes, ____________

4 Present progressive or present simple in context. Put in the right form of the verb in brackets.

LAURA Hello, George! What [1]____ (you/do) these days?
GEORGE Hi, Laura. I [2]____ (learn) French and Spanish at college. What about you?
LAURA Me? Oh, I [3]____ (work) at a Travel Agency until August.
GEORGE [4]____ (you/like) it?
LAURA Yes, I do. They [5]____ (give) me quite a good training. I [6]____ (work) in the shop most mornings, and three afternoons a week the manager [7]____ (tell) me about the travel business. I [8]____ (work) quite long hours. I [9]____ (not/get) home until six, but I [10]____ (prefer) that to not having enough to do.
GEORGE Yes, I [11]____ (work) hard too at the moment. It [12]____ (become) more and more difficult to get a job using languages. They [13]____ (ask) for higher and higher exam grades all the time.
LAURA You can do it, George. You [14]____ (be) clever.
GEORGE Thanks, Laura.

2

Offers, suggestions and asking for advice: *will, shall, can* etc.

A Starting activities

1 I'll make my bed but not yours

Offers with *will*

Work in pairs, A and B. You and your partner share a flat. Think of household chores that you always do that you would like your partner to help with. Take it in turns to be A. A asks for help (in any way) and B offers to help, using *will*. B offers to do a part of the job or to do it on certain days only.

Examples:

A: *I'd like some help making the beds.*

B: *I'll make my bed but not yours.*

A: *Can you help with the washing up sometimes, please?*

B: *I'll do it from Monday to Friday but not at the weekends.*

2 Shall we go to Alexander's?

Suggestions with *shall*

Work in pairs, A and B. Both secretly write down the name of the place you would most like to go to tomorrow evening (cinema, theatre, restaurant, nightclub, disco, café – anywhere you like). Take it in turns to be A. A tries to find out what B has written down by making suggestions with *shall*. B can help A to guess by giving clues, like this:

A: *Shall we go to Alexander's, the new nightclub?*

B: *No, I don't like noisy places.*

A: *Shall we go to a quiet restaurant then?*

B: *No, . . .*

3 Why don't we get the President a new helicopter?

Suggestions with *Let's, Why don't we?, How about?* and *What about?*

Work as a class. Make suggestions about what to buy well-known people for their birthday. Use *Let's, Why don't we?, How about?* and *What about?*

Example: *Why don't we get the President a new helicopter?*

Here are some ideas for presents:

Leisure items: a guitar, a book about . . ., a computer game

Luxury items: a new sports car, a swimming pool, an expensive suit or dress

Practical and useful items: a burglar alarm, a pram for the baby, a pair of socks or tights, a shirt or a blouse

4 Getting them clear

Offers, suggestions and asking for advice

Work in pairs or as a class. Say which of these sentences are offers, which are suggestions, and which are asking for advice. Say whether they are formal or informal. Use the Grammar guide to help you, if you need to.

1 Would you like us to wait for you?
2 What shall we do if it rains?
3 You could leave it until later.
4 I can easily repair that for you, if you like.
5 Let's tell Gavin what's happened.

When you have finished, look at Activity note 17 on page 140.

B Grammar guide

1 Offers

- Use *I'll* in informal English to say that you are willing to do something (you are offering to do something). *I'll* is sometimes used with the phrase *if you like* (or *if you want*).
  I'll do the washing up, if you like.
- Use *shall I?* or *shall we?* in informal English to offer to help. *Shall I?* or *shall we?* means 'do you want me/us to?'. *Shall* is not usually used with *you, he, she, it* or *they.*
  Shall I do the washing up?
- You can also use *I can* or *can I?* in informal English to offer to help. Like *I'll, I can* is sometimes used with *if you like/want.*
  I can drop you off at the station, if you want.
  Can I give you a lift?
- *I could, could I?* and *would you like me to?* are more formal than *can* and *I'll.* You can use *could,* like *can,* in positive sentences or as a question to offer to help. *I could* is sometimes used with *if you like/wish.*
  I could book the tickets for you (if you like).
  Could I book the tickets for you?
  Could John go to the supermarket for you?
  Would you like me to meet you at the station?

2 Suggestions and asking for advice

- In informal English we use *shall I/we?* to make suggestions or to ask for advice. We use *shall* with *I* and *we* only.
  Shall we go to the café afterwards? (suggestion)
  What shall we do? (asking for advice)
- Use *can* or *could* for suggestions, especially with *if you like/want.* This is informal English.
  We can go and see John, if you like.
  You could leave a note.
  I could meet you at the station.
- *Let's, Why don't you/we?, How about?* and *What about?* are all used to make suggestions in informal English. *Let's* and *Why don't you/we?* are followed by the infinitive without *to.*
  Let's have a picnic.
  Why don't we play tennis?
  How about? and *What about?* are followed by an *-ing* form or a noun.
  How about going to the park?
  What about the disco?

C Activities

1 Helping a disabled person

Offers and suggestions

1 Work as a class. List things that disabled people need help with. Include things that people in wheelchairs and blind and deaf people need help with; for example, shopping, cleaning the house, getting dressed.

2 Work in pairs. Imagine that you are a disabled person (a blind or deaf person, or someone in a wheelchair). Make a day-by-day timetable of things that you need help with, as well as some things where no help is needed. Both of you should write the timetable, like this:
Monday: Help with washing and drying clothes.
No help needed to clean the house.

3 Change pairs. Take it in turns to make offers of help to the disabled person. Accept or reject the help according to what you have written on your list. Example:
A: *Would you like me to help you to clean the house?*
B: *No, thanks. (I can manage.)*
Is there anything on your list that you have not received an offer of help about? If there is, say 'I also need help with . . .' and the other person will make another offer of help, and arrange a time to do it. Example:
A: *I also need help with washing and drying clothes.*
B: *Shall I do that for you? What about Monday?*
A: *Yes, Monday is fine.*

2 Homeless

will **for offers,** ***shall*** **for asking for advice and making suggestions**

Work in pairs, A and B. Decide who is A and who is B. There was a disaster in your area. (Flood? Earthquake? Decide what kind of disaster it was.) A family has suddenly been made homeless in the middle of the night and they have probably lost everything that was in their home. There is a mother and father, a grandfather, a daughter aged two and a son aged nine. (How do they feel?)
Person A: Read Activity note 18 on page 141.
Person B: Read Activity note 55 on page 154.

3 The coffee room

Suggestions

1 Work in pairs or groups. You are staff and students who are chatting informally in the coffee room. You are talking about your English lessons and suggesting changes. For example, you can suggest changes in these areas: the timetable, the breaks (more/fewer breaks? shorter/longer breaks?), the type of lessons (more grammar? less grammar?), the length of lessons, the number of lessons per week, the amount of homework (more/less?). Somebody could suggest a 'partner' scheme where students who find English easy to learn help students who find it more difficult. Example: *We could have some short lessons and some long lessons.*

2 Say your suggestions to the class and discuss other people's suggestions. Write down the best suggestions.

D Accuracy practice

1 **Use *I could* or *Would you like me to?* to complete these formal offers from the Director's Personal Assistant.**

1 ____ give the report to Mrs Toner while you are in the meeting?
2 There are no direct flights but ____ book one via Dubai, if you like.
3 ____ type the letters and post them for you on my way home?
4 ____ cancel your eleven o'clock appointment, if you wish.
5 ____ start a new file for each eastern European country?

2 **Use *shall, will* or *can* to complete these informal offers. Sometimes more than one answer is possible.**

1 A friend is trying to move a heavy piece of furniture.
'____ give you a hand?'
2 There is a lot of washing up to do.
'You do the washing up and ____ do the drying.'
3 A friend is taking some CDs next door. You are going there anyway.
'____ take them next door for you, if you like.'
4 You are in an old lady's front room. She has some letters on her table, addressed and with stamps on them.
'____ post those letters for you, if you want.'
5 Andrew is looking helplessly at an old-fashioned tin opener. You know how to use it.
'Andrew, ____ open that tin for you?'

3 **Use *shall, can, Let's, Why don't?* or *How about?* to make suggestions in informal English.**

1 You ____ have the party at our place, if you want to.
2 ____ playing basketball after the lesson?
3 ____ you get yourself a new pair of jeans? You can afford to.
4 ____ I go and ask at Reception whether there is a spare key to the room?
5 ____ try to book the trip to the lakes now.
6 ____ you ask the bank for a bigger loan?
7 ____ we go to the club this evening?
8 ____ helping Diane with some of her homework?
9 'Who else could we invite?' '____ Charlie and Ethel Smith?'
10 You ____ come with me, and Robert ____ go with Tessa.

4 **These offers, suggestions and requests for advice are wrong. Correct them.**

1 ~~Why don't we going to the cinema?~~
2 ~~How about we play tennis?~~
3 ~~Shall Phil get the tickets for you? He doesn't mind standing in a queue.~~
4 ~~Would I take those boxes for you?~~
5 ~~I help you with the coffee?~~

3

Prepositions of position, movement and time

A Starting activities

1 Sorting them out

Prepositions of position, movement and time

1 Work as a class. Classify the words below into prepositions of position, movement and time. Some come into more than one category.
in, at, on, onto, into, along, during

When you have finished look at Activity note 61 on page 156.

2 Work as a class. Think of sentences:
a that include *in* as a preposition of position, movement and time (3 sentences),
b that include *at* as a preposition of position and time (2 sentences),
c that include *on* as a preposition of position, movement and time (3 sentences).
Example: *The wine is in the cellar.* (*in* for position)

2 The first person to build a house on the moon

Prepositions of time

1 Work in pairs. Write a paragraph about the first person to build a house on the moon. Use these phrases to help you:
s/he was born at . . . o'clock on the . . . of . . .
before starting . . .
after leaving . . .
until s/he was 19 s/he had never . . .
by the time s/he was 25 s/he had . . .
from . . . to . . . s/he was a . . .
for . . . years s/he . . . and during this time s/he . . .
in the winter of . . . s/he . . .

2 Work as a class. Read your paragraph to the class and listen to other people's paragraphs, writing down any uses of prepositions you did not know before.

3 After the party

Prepositions of position and movement

1 Work in pairs, A and B. Make a quick, large copy of this drawing of a family living room.

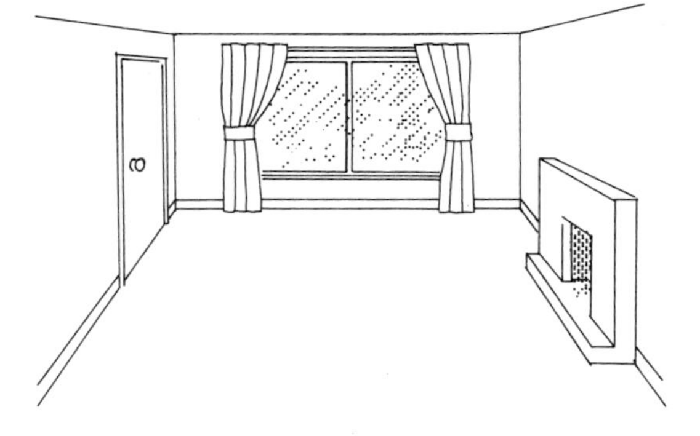

Discuss and agree on where all the furnishings listed below should go using the prepositions of position.
Example: *Let's put a picture above the fireplace.*
Furnishings: two armchairs, a small round table, a large square table, a sofa, a television set, a rug, pictures on the walls, a table lamp, a light, ashtrays, a poster, some books, a piano, a bookcase. (Put in anything else that you both want to.)
Prepositions of position: *above, behind, beside, between, in* (*in the middle, in this corner*), *in front of, near, on, on top of, under*

2 Now decide who is A and who is B. A is sixteen years old and B is A's mother or father. Last night A had a party for all his or her friends. The living room now looks quite different.
Person A: Read Activity note 36 on page 146.
Person B: Read Activity note 69 on page 159.

B Grammar guide

1 Prepositions of position

The car is in front of the lorry.

A suitcase is on top of the car.

The lorry is behind the car.

Jim is standing by (or *beside*) *his car.*

The picture is above (or *over*) *the clock.*

The clock is under the picture.

- *At* is used for location. (*at the top of the page, at the bus stop*)
- *On* is used when something is touching a surface (*on a noticeboard*). It is used in some position phrases (*on the right*), in some geographical expressions (*on the coast*) and in some 'parts of the body' expressions. (*He had a funny look on his face.*)
- *In* is used when someone or something is surrounded on all sides (*in the newspaper, in the street*). Note that with cities and countries we use *in* (*I live in Oxford.*) but with addresses we use *at* (*I live at 15 Royal Street.*).
- Other prepositions of position: *between, close to, near, next to* and *opposite.*

2 Prepositions of movement

- Use *into* and *onto* with movement verbs. (*He drove into the car park.*) But with some movement verbs we normally use *in* instead of *into* and *on* instead of *onto*. The most common of these are *drop, fall, jump, put* and *throw.*
- Most of the prepositions of position in 1 are also prepositions of movement. *She ran behind the tree.* *The plane flew over the city.*
- Other prepositions of movement: *along, across, around, round* and *through.*

3 Prepositions of time

- *At* is used with times (*at five o'clock, at night, at the weekend*) and also with festivals (*at Christmas* means the period of the Christmas holiday).
- *On* is used with days, including single days of festivals (*on Friday, on Sunday morning, on Christmas Day*). Note also *on holiday.*
- *In* is used for 'within' periods of time (*in May, in the evening, in 1998*) and for how long something took. (*She learned English in six months.*)
- Use *during* to say when something happened. *During* is followed by a noun. (*There was a thunderstorm during the night.*) Use *for* to answer the question 'how long?'. (*We worked on the house for six months.*)
- You can talk about a length of time using *from . . . to.* (*The film went on from seven-thirty to ten o'clock.*)
- Use *by* for 'not later than (a point of time)'. (*I'll tell you by Monday* = on or before Monday.) Use *until* to mean 'between two points of time'. (*You have until Monday to tell me.* = You have all the time before Monday to tell me.)
- Other prepositions of time include *before* and *after.* (*After leaving school she got a job as a journalist.*)

C Activities

1 Every picture tells a story

Prepositions of position and movement

1 Work as a class. You need a piece of paper large enough to draw a picture on. (Don't worry if you can't draw very well. It doesn't matter.) Your teacher will read a description of a picture from Activity note 37 on page 146. (The description is for the teacher only.) The description of the picture will include these prepositions: *in, at, on, into, off, above, from, to, by, over, beside, along, under.* You draw the picture as your teacher describes it. Your teacher will read the description more than once, if necessary, and you can look at what other people are drawing, if you need to. Keep your picture when it is finished, because you will need it for the next activity (called 'Storyboard').

2 Work as a class. Your teacher will ask one person from the class to come to the board, without the picture. The rest of the class describes the picture while the person at the board draws it again on the board. Check that the picture is correct and list any prepositions that you want to remember.

2 Storyboard

Prepositions of position and movement

1 Work in pairs or small groups. You are going to prepare a storyboard. A storyboard is drawn before a film is made. It is made up of drawings of all the scenes in the film. Your storyboard can have three, four, five or six pictures in it. One of the pictures in the storyboard will be the one you drew in Activity 1. You can put it in any position in the storyboard. The storyboard is called 'A child is saved from drowning'. Decide what should go in each picture of the storyboard and then one person draws it. (It does not matter how good or bad the drawing is.) If you want to, you can also write captions for each picture and write speech coming out of the mouths of people in the story. Use as many prepositions of position and movement as you realistically can.
Example:
The man ran over the bridge and along the riverbank, dived into the water and swam to the boy.

2 Work in pairs, small groups or as a class. Explain your storyboard to another pair or group or to the class. List any interesting uses of prepositions of place and movement from other people's storyboards.

3 Pickpockets

Prepositions of position and movement

1 Work in pairs or in three groups. Three pickpockets stole a wallet outside the school where you are learning English. Your class saw them and chased them right across the town. Later you told the police what happened. Use all the prepositions below and as many of the verbs as you like to help you. Describe what happened when you chased either Pickpocket 1 or Pickpocket 2 or Pickpocket 3.
Example: *She ran across the main square and disappeared into a café.*

Pickpocket 1 was a woman in a red dress. You chased her across town on foot.

Pickpocket 2 was a man in his mid-twenties. He got away in a car. You chased him in a car.

Pickpocket 3 was a middle-aged woman. She started off on foot, then caught a bus and then a train. You chased her all the way.

Prepositions: *across, along, around, away from, behind, beside, down, from, inside, into, near, off, onto, out of, round, through, to, towards, up*

Verbs: *run, turn, go, drive, disappear, scramble, walk, slip*

2 Work as a class. Tell the class about your chase and list prepositions and verbs from other people's chase stories.

D Accuracy practice

1 ***In, at* or *on*? Put in the correct prepositions of position.**

1 I was standing ____ the bus stop ____ the end of the street.
2 You can often see birds ____ the grass ____ the park opposite my house.
3 I saw your name ____ the office door. Are you the Geoffrey Henderson whose picture has been ____ the paper?
4 We were ____ Paris, on holiday, and ran into her ____ the street.
5 Pin the notice up ____ the noticeboard, ____ the top.

2 ***In* or *into*, *on* or *onto*? Put in the correct prepositions of movement.**

1 Put the orange juice ____ the fridge, ____ the bottom shelf, please.
2 I hurt my back lifting those cases ____ the boot of the car.
3 As he put the tray ____ the table he dropped one of the knives ____ the floor.
4 A bird flew ____ my room this morning and then flew right ____ the top of the cupboard.
5 He came ____ the room angrily and threw his briefcase ____ the desk.

3 ***In, at, on, from . . . to, for* or *during*? Put in the correct prepositions of time.**

1 I never see that cat ____ the day. I think it only comes out ____ night.
2 They got married ____ the spring, ____ 1993.
3 She works late ____ Mondays and gets home ____ seven ____ the evening.
4 Joyce has been playing her guitar ____ three hours now. Sometimes she plays ____ early morning ____ late ____ the afternoon.
5 She never sends cards ____ Christmas and one year she just turned up without warning ____ Christmas Day.
6 I saw her ____ the weekend, or was it some time ____ the week?
7 It doesn't rain much ____ July so we usually go on holiday ____ that time of year.

4 **Complete these sentences using *by* or *until*.**

1 I can't take any more time off work ____ next year, I'm afraid.
2 We have to finish writing this ____ three o'clock.
3 Fasten your seatbelt, please, madam, and you'll have to finish your meal ____ the time we land.
4 I don't really want to switch the television off ____ the programme finishes.
5 You're late, we should have started ____ now.

4

Past progressive and past simple

A Starting activities

1 What were you doing?

Past progressive

1 Work in pairs. Ask your partner questions about what he or she was doing every hour yesterday morning (from eight o'clock to twelve o'clock). Take turns to ask and answer. Use the past progressive, like this:
A: *What were you doing at eight o'clock yesterday morning?*
B: *I was getting dressed.*

2 Make a list of the things you were both doing at the same time.
At eight o'clock we were both getting dressed.

2 Cinderella, all wrong

Past simple

Work in pairs or small groups. One person in each pair or group reads the story of Cinderella aloud. Every time you hear something wrong, stop the story and correct the mistake, using a past simple negative, like this: *No, Cinderella wasn't a man, she was a woman.* (If you don't know the story of Cinderella, read Activity note 7 on page 138 before you start.)

Cinderella
Cinderella was a young man who lived with her stepmother and her two beautiful sisters. Cinderella made the two sisters do all the work around the house and she wore beautiful clothes while her two sisters went around in rags. One day there was a ball at the palace and an ugly fairy godmother appeared and told Cinderella that she could go to the ball – but she had to be back by half-past seven. So Cinderella went to the ball and danced with the short fat prince. As she left she dropped her football boot on the stairs. The next day the prince searched everywhere for Cinderella and when he found her he gave her a job in the palace kitchen.

3 Some questions

Use of the past progressive and past simple

Work as a class.

1 Sentence 1: *I was having lunch at the café when I saw John in the street.*
Sentence 2: *I had lunch at the café and then I saw John in the street.*
a Had I finished lunch when I saw John in sentence 1?
b Had I finished lunch when I saw John in sentence 2?

2 *I was walking along the street when I* (verb) . . .
a *I was walking* is past progressive. Which tense do you think the missing verb will be?
b Can you start the sentence *When I* (verb) . . . ? In other words can you turn the sentence round?

3 *I was driving to London when the accident happened.*
There are two actions in this sentence, driving to London and the accident happening. Which of the two actions do you think the speaker sees as the most important one and which one is the 'background' action (the less important one)?

When you have finished look at Activity note 3 on page 136.

B Grammar guide

1 Past progressive

We use the past PROGRESSive when we refer to something that was happening (that is, it was in PROGRESS) at a definite time in the past.
At one o'clock yesterday I was having lunch.

- We can use *while* and *when* to join two actions which were happening at the same time in the past. Both actions have a past progressive verb.
  He was doing the shopping while I was parking the car.
- We can use *still* to emphasize that something was continuing, especially after the time it was expected to finish.
  At a quarter-past ten I was still waiting for the train.

2 Past simple

We use the past simple when we refer to a finished action or situation in the past.
We use the past simple to talk about:

- finished single actions or situations:
  I went to London yesterday.
  I lived in London when I was a child.
- finished repeated actions or situations:
  Every year when I was a child we went to Italy on holiday.
  When she was young she lived in a different country every year.

NOTE State verbs are usually used in the past simple and not in the past progressive.
I was running home. I knew I was late. NOT ~~*was knowing*~~

NOTE *Ago* means 'at some time before now'. It is usually used with the past simple.
I lived there ten years ago.

3 Past progressive and past simple in context

When we use the past progressive and the past simple together, we can use the past progressive to 'paint a picture' of a longer 'background' action. We use the past simple for what the speaker sees as the main action in the past.
We were living in London when Susan made her first film.
We went indoors because it was raining.

- If there is more than one 'background' action, do not repeat *was/were* for the second or third action.
  The teachers were sitting in the staff room, marking books and drinking coffee when I came in. (NOT ~~*were marking books and were drinking coffee*~~)
- You can use *while, as, when* and *whenever* to introduce the longer 'background' action. *While* and *as* mean 'at the same time as'. *When* tells you which time and *whenever* means 'every time'.
  As/While I was driving to Oxford I saw a tiny little house with no roof.
  When I was sitting on the beach I saw a ship in the distance.
  He went to see Jennifer whenever he was visiting Oxford.
- You can use *just* to emphasize that the longer action had only recently started when the action in the past simple interrupted it.
  I was just leaving when she asked me to stay.

C Activities

1 Some funny things happened

Past progressive and past simple

1 Work in pairs, A and B. Yesterday you and your partner were in a shop. (Decide together what kind of shop you were in.) Some unusual things happened.
Person A: Read Activity note 6 on page 137.
Person B: Read Activity note 44 on page 149.

2 Work in the same pairs or join with another pair to make a group of four. Choose one of your sentences from 1 and use it at the beginning, in the middle or at the end of an anecdote (a short funny story) about what happened in the shop. Use as many past simple and past progressive sentences in the anecdote as you naturally can.

3 Tell your anecdote to the class. List any interesting sentences with the past simple or past progressive from other people's stories.

2 An interview

Past progressive and past simple

1 Work in pairs. Choose a famous person you both know about, or choose someone from the 'Notes about famous people' in Activity note 45 on page 149. Working together, write sentences about the famous person using the structures below. Example: *While she was working as a model she met Roger Vadim, the film director.*

Structures
while + past progressive
(*While she/he was . . . ing . . .*)
when + past progressive
(*When she/he was . . . ing . . .*)
past simple + *years ago* (*She/he . . . years ago.*)
in (year) + past simple (*In . . . she/he . . .*)
from (year) *to* (year) (*She/he . . . from . . . to . . .*)

2 Work in the same pairs. One of you is an interviewer and the other is the famous person you wrote the sentences about in 1. The interviewer asks the famous person about his or her life and work. Use the structures from 1 in the questions and the answers, like this: *What did your husband do while you were making films?* Use as many past simple and past progressive sentences as you naturally can.

3 Every picture tells a story

Past progressive and past simple

1 Work in pairs or groups. Look at the drawings below. For each of the four pictures write two 'background' sentences on a piece of paper using the past progressive. Leave plenty of space underneath the sentences for each picture. Examples: *The sun was shining. Geraldine and Mike were coming home from work.*

2 Under the two background sentences, write the beginning of each of the four stories (two or three sentences each) using the past simple. Example: *Geraldine heard a loud noise.*

3 Number the stories 1 to 4, then pass your work to another pair or group to continue the stories. Pass the paper on after you have written two or three sentences each time.

4 When all the stories are complete, read them to the whole class. Correct any mistakes.

D Accuracy practice

1 Write sentences. Use the past progressive in a positive, negative or question form.

1 /you/use/the hairdrier/when the lights went out?
2 /John/not talk/to Barbara. Barbara was not even in the room.
3 The last time I saw him,/Dick/drink/orange juice in the kitchen.
4 /you/drive/slowly/when you saw the man in the road?
5 /It/snow/as I left home for the last time.

2 Rewrite the sentences. Use the past progressive and past simple with *when* or *while*.

1 Before the bus had completely stopped, the child jumped off.
The bus ______________
2 As Jane wrote the last sentence of her homework, her friend asked her to do his as well.
Jane was ______________
3 During dinner at Harry's Anna lost her necklace.
While Anna ______________
4 John brought the sweet in but I still had some chips on my plate to eat.
I was still ______________
5 Did Emily wear that dress when she got married?
Was Emily ______________ ?

3 Join the sentences using *as, just, while, when* and *ago*. Put the verbs into the past progressive or the past simple.

1 I (eat) my dinner. There (be) a knock at the door. (AS)
2 Camilla (get) into the car. Henry (shout) a warning. (JUST, WHEN)
3 You (dance) at the disco. I (paint) the kitchen at home. (WHILE)
4 I (know) her ten years. She (work) for Star Electronics at the same time as I was. (AGO, WHEN)
5 James (hear) a noise. He (listen to) the music. (WHILE)

4 Past progressive or past simple in context. Put in the right form of the verb in brackets. Sometimes either form is possible.

I [1]____ (walk) along the street one day when I [2]____ (see) something very strange. I [3]____ (notice) a man the same height as me who [4]____ (have) a beard like mine. He [5]____ (wear) a blue shirt and an old pair of jeans and he [6]____ (carry) a bag with some books in it. He [7]____ (just/cross) the road ahead of me but he [8]____ (not/avoid) me deliberately, I [9]____ (be) sure of that. As he [10]____ (go across) the road I [11]____ (follow) him. I [12]____ (wonder) whether or not to stop him and ask him whether he had noticed something strange too. I [13]____ (still/think) about it when he [14]____ (turn round) suddenly and we [15]____ (look at) each other. He [16]____ (look) amazed. 'It's unbelievable, isn't it?' I [17]____ (say) as I [18]____ (stare at) his face, which [19]____ (be) just like mine, and at his hair, which [20]____ (also/be) just like mine. 'You are my double. You look exactly the same as me.'

5

Habit: *used to, would, will*

A Starting activities

1 What a good child

***used to* for repeated or regular actions in the past**

1 Work in pairs. Persuade your partner that you were a model, perfect child. Use imaginary or real memories from your childhood which show how perfect you were. Say sentences with *used to*, like this: *When I was a child I used to help my parents clean the house every day.*

2 Work as a class. Say your sentences to the class. Who was the most perfect child in the class?

2 Epitaphs for animals

***would* for repeated or regular actions in the past**

1 Work with a partner. An epitaph is written on the gravestone of someone who has died. Imagine that you are writing an epitaph for an animal that you had as a pet, or that lived on a farm near you. Use the list of verbs below to help you. Choose three animals. Write sentences saying what each animal would always do when it was alive, like this: *He would always let me ride on his back.*
Animals: horse, donkey, dog, cat, bird, cow, sheep, chicken
Verbs: *sing, lay* (eggs), *give, play, follow, obey, bark, purr, stroke, carry, sleep, chase*

2 Read some of your epitaphs to the class. Write down the most moving, interesting or funny epitaphs you hear.

3 Why are these wrong?

used to, would* and *will

Work as a class. Which of the *information sentences* (a–e) tells you why each of the *wrong sentences* (1, 2 and 3) is wrong?

Wrong sentences

1 ~~When I was a young man I would have a moustache.~~
2 ~~Maria used to learn English for five years.~~
3 ~~She'll keep bringing friends home to dinner without telling me in advance.~~

Information sentences

a Don't use *used to* to talk about the total number of times something happened.
b Don't use *used to* to talk about how long something went on for.
c Don't use *would* for past states or situations (only past actions).
d Use *would* stressed to criticize typical action or behaviour in the past.
e We cannot use the short form of *will* to suggest criticism, because *will* must be stressed.

When you have finished, look at Activity note 19 on page 141.

B Grammar guide

1 *used to*

- *Used to* only exists in the simple past tense. Ask questions with *Did you use to . . . ?* The negative is *I did not use to . . .* or *I never used to . . . .*
- Use *used to* to talk about:

a repeated or regular actions in the past which do not happen now:
When I was twelve I used to go to the cinema every week.
NOTE This use of *used to* is useful for contrasting the past generally with the present generally, especially when talking about attitudes and behaviour.
People didn't use to put their relatives in old people's homes but they do now.

b past states which are not true now:
I used to have black hair but it's gone grey now.

c past situations which are not the situation now:
He used to be Mary's boyfriend but now he's Rachel's.

- Don't use *used to*:

a a second time after *and* (or *when, while*):
I used to go to the cinema every week and sit in the front row. (NOT ~~*used to sit*~~)

b to talk about how long something went on for (use the past simple):
I went to that school for five years. (NOT ~~*used to go*~~)

c to talk about the number of times something happened (use the past simple):
We went there on holiday five times. (NOT ~~*used to go*~~)

2 *would*

- *Would* is followed by the infinitive without *to*. It can be contracted to *I'd, you'd, she'd* and so on. The negative is *I would not* or *I would never.*
- *Would* is often more formal than *used to*. Use *would* to:

a talk about repeated or regular actions in the past which do not happen now (the same use as *used to*):
In his youth he would go to the cinema every week.
NOTE As with *used to*, this use of *would* is useful for contrasting the past generally with the present generally.
In the old days people would help you if you were in trouble, but they won't now.

b make criticisms of somebody's behaviour:
She ***would*** *leave my umbrella on the bus.*
In this use, *would* is stressed. It can be used for a single action, but one that is typical of somebody.

- We don't use *would* for past states or situations (only for past actions). So you can say *I used to have black hair* but you cannot say ~~*I would have black hair.*~~

3 *will*

- *Will* + infinitive without *to* is used for a person's typical behaviour now.
He'll watch television for hours in the evening.
- As with *would*, if you stress *will* it suggests criticism. *Will* + infinitive without *to* is used for repeated action, suggesting criticism.
He ***will*** *forget to lock the door when he goes out.*
The short forms *I'll, he'll*, etc. are not possible here because *will* must be stressed.

C Activities

1 Older and wiser

used to, didn't use to

1 Work alone. Write *used to* and *didn't use to* sentences for every year of your life between the ages of six and sixteen, like this: *When I was fifteen I used to eat a lot more than I do now. When I was sixteen I didn't use to fall in love as easily as I do now.*

2 Work in pairs. Compare your sentences with the person next to you.

2 He used to make me do too much work

used to* and *would

1 Work alone. A newspaper phones you for information about someone from your past. Choose someone you used to know well but who you do not see any more. It could be someone you liked or a person you disliked. Prepare enough information to speak for three or four minutes over the phone. Use as many *used to* and *would* sentences as you realistically can. Example:
Mr Jones was my English teacher at school. He used to make me angry. He would always make me do more work than I wanted to do.

2 Work in pairs, groups or as a class. Give your information about the person you used to know well as if you were speaking on the phone. Speak for three or four minutes.

3 He will make films about aliens

***will* and *would* for criticism**

1 Work as a class. Say sentences critical of the behaviour of the people below. Use *will* for present behaviour and *would* for past behaviour. Stress *will* and *would*, like this: *He* ***will*** *make films about aliens all the time. He* ***would*** *move his hips while he was singing.*
People: Stephen Spielberg, Elvis Presley, Michael Jackson, Pablo Picasso.

2 Work in pairs or groups. Think of more *will* (present behaviour) and *would* (past behaviour) sentences for people you think the whole class will know or know of. You will need your sentences for 3.

3 Work as a class. Say your *will* or *would* sentences to the class for them to guess who the sentences are about. Guess who other people's sentences are about.

4 The good old days?

***used to, would* and *will* in past/present contrasts**

Work as a class. Discuss how the world has changed since your grandparents' time. Contrast that past time with the way we live today, like this: *People used to stop and help if your car broke down, but they won't help you today. In the past a man would give up his seat to a woman on a bus or a train. Young men today won't do that.*

Has the world got better or worse? Discuss transport, behaviour with strangers, neighbours, writing letters, local shops and supermarkets, boyfriends and girlfriends, comfort, machines, travel and health.

D Accuracy practice

1 **WHERE POSSIBLE, rewrite these sentences using *would* instead of the first verb in the past simple.**

1 I went to Tokyo last year.
2 He met her every time she came to Madrid.
3 I went swimming twice a day when we lived on the coast.
4 She wrote to me for three years and then stopped.
5 Richard asked Laura three times if she wanted to come.
6 When she lived at home, Laura borrowed her parents' car to drive into town.
7 We left our cat with the neighbours when we went on holiday.

2 **Complete the sentences using *used to* (positive, negative, or question).**

1 ____ (you) play with your brother's toys when you were young?
2 I never ____ eat so much in the evenings!
3 I ____ (not) go out much until I was twenty.
4 Sarah ____ (not) be as clever as Ray but she is now.
5 I can remember, darling, how we ____ walk home holding hands.
6 There ____ be a hotel where the Town Hall is now.
7 ____ (you) play football when you were at school?
8 Who ____ be the first to help when someone was in trouble?

3 **These sentences are wrong. Correct them.**

1 Last week I used to go to London.
2 I often used to see Peter when we used to be in the same football team.
3 Sheila used to write to me for six months.
4 When I was young I would have only three smart shirts.
5 He'll eat with his mouth open, which is very irritating.

4 **Change any past tense verbs that can be changed to *used to* or *would* + infinitive. Change present tense verbs that can be changed to *will* + infinitive.**

Doyle had a hard childhood because Glasgow (1) *was* a hard city. He (2) *got up* every day while it (3) *was* still dark. His day (4) *began* with stealing milk from outside people's front doors and sometimes he (5) *stole* newspapers too. He (6) *threw* them all over the wet streets just as the sun was rising over the tops of the factories. He (7) *was* a bad boy, as he (8) *tells* journalists and anybody else who will listen to him, sitting at his regular table at his favourite bar in the centre of the city. He (9) *tells* you his stories every evening. He has stories about how he (10) *drove* to the coast in stolen cars, how he (11) *got into* fights, and how one day the police (12) *arrested* him and (13) *put* him in prison. And, of course, he (14) *tells* you the well-known story of how he (15) *learned* to paint in prison.

6

Question forms and question tags

A Starting activities

1 Finding the question

Types of question

1 Work in pairs. Here are some answers to questions. Think of as many questions as you can for each answer. Example: 1 *What is the capital of England?* Use the categories in 2 below to help you if necessary.

1	London.	6	Yes.
2	No, never.	7	Yes, he is.
3	No, they don't.	8	On Saturday.
4	I'm not sure.	9	No, she doesn't have to.
5	Yes, I do sometimes.	10	Yes, I have.

2 Work as a class. Say some of your questions to the class. Which of the categories (a–f below) do the questions come into?

Categories

Questions beginning with:

a *do, does* or *did*
b *am, is* or *are*
c *have* or *has*
d a modal verb (like *can*)
e a question word (like *what, how, whose*)
f a phrase like *Is it true that . . ., Can you tell me . .*

2 I'm surprised

Questions with statement word order to show surprise

1 Work on your own. Write down something surprising about the person on your right. If you don't know anything surprising, make something up. Examples: *Carlos has five children. Peter is a millionaire.*

2 Pass what you have written to the person on your left. Read out to the class the information passed to you. Sound as surprised as you can. Examples: *CARlos has FIVE CHILdren? PEter is a MILLionAIRE?*

3 This is about question tags, isn't it?

Question tags

Work in pairs. Take it in turns to make statements with question tags. Use the information and the question tags below. Example: 1 *It's a nice day, isn't it?*

Information

1 You think it's a nice day.
2 You think the supermarket sells newspapers.
3 You think you are late.
4 You think Tom doesn't like soup.
5 You think Diane has read 'War and Peace'.
6 You think Dick and Tina went camping last year.
7 You think old Mrs Pearson hasn't been well lately.
8 You think Margaret isn't playing tennis tomorrow.
9 You think Dick wasn't there when Joy came.
10 You think Mr Sanders hasn't been telling the truth.

Question tags

aren't I?	was he?	isn't she?	isn't it?
has she?	does he?	doesn't it?	has he?
didn't they?	hasn't she?	is she?	

When you have finished, look at Activity note 31 on page 145.

B Grammar guide

1 Yes/no questions

- Yes/no questions are questions that can be answered by *yes* or *no*. This is the word order for yes/no questions:

Auxiliary	Subject	Main verb	
Is	*John*	*coming?*	
Have	*you*	*met*	*Rachel?*
Can	*Peter*	*ride*	*a bike?*

- The present simple and past simple tenses do not have an auxiliary (*be, have* or a modal verb like *can*), so in the present simple tense use *do/does* before the subject to make a question. In the past simple use *did.*
  Do you like chicken? *Does Martin live here?* *Did the train leave on time?*

2 Wh- questions

- Wh- questions begin with a question word (*how, what, where, when, who, whose, which* or *why*).
  Where's Kerry? *Whose bag is this?*
  How can go before words like *big, far, long, often, much* and *many.*
  How far is it to the station from here?
- When *who, what, which* or *whose* is the subject, it comes directly before the verb, as in a statement.
  Who put that on my desk? (like the statement *Sheila put that on my desk.*)
  When *who, what, which* or *whose* is the object, an auxiliary comes before the subject.
  What did Sheila put on my desk?

3 Negative questions

You can use negative questions to make suggestions or when you expect the listener to agree with you (to say 'yes').
Why don't we go to the park? (suggestion)
Aren't you Jim's brother? (expecting the answer 'yes')

4 Questions with statement word order

- To show surprise you can say a question with a statement word order.
  You're coming with us after all?
- In indirect questions the word order after the question word is the same as in statements.
  Can you tell me where Tom is? (NOT ~~*where is Tom*~~)

5 Question tags

- Use question tags to ask for agreement or confirmation. Usually, positive statements have negative question tags and negative statements have positive question tags. The question tag usually uses the same auxiliary verb as the statement.
  He hasn't got any money, has he? *He has got some money, hasn't he?*
  They couldn't lose, could they?
- There are 'same way' question tags which express interest or surprise.
  Oh, you're Jim's brother, are you?
- The question tag after *let's* is *shall.* After the imperative the tag is *will you.*
  Let's ask Jane, shall we? *Don't tell Maria, will you?*

C Activities

1 How honest are you?

Question forms

1 Work in pairs or groups. Write a questionnaire to find out how honest people in the class are. Use any questions of your own that you like but include at least one of the following question forms:
Have you ever . . .?
How would you react if. . .?
What would you do if. . .?
Which of the following do you think is morally wrong? (Use an *-ing* form for your examples, like this: *Leaving a shop without paying.*)

2 Ask people your questions.

3 Report the answers to the class and say how honest you think the class is.

2 When are you free to start?

Yes/no and wh- questions

1 Work as a class. List questions that employers ask at job interviews. Examples: *Why do you want this job? Are you free to start immediately?* Then list questions that applicants ask at job interviews. Examples: *What are the hours of work? How long are the holidays?*

2 Work in pairs. Decide which jobs you are applying for. Take it in turns to interview each other for jobs. Use the questions you have already listed and some questions specific to the particular job you are applying for. Example: *Why are you interested in nursing?* You can choose any jobs you like but there are some suggestions below.

Jobs: nurse, secretary, builder, bank clerk, teacher, journalist, lawyer, astronaut, computer programmer, actor/actress, television presenter

3 Hamlet arrested!

Wh- questions

1 Work as a class. Imagine that a character from a fairy story, a myth, a film, a play or a novel has been arrested by the police. Choose a character from a story that the class knows well. List one or two wh- questions that the police might ask. For example, in the play 'Hamlet', Hamlet kills Polonius and Ophelia drowns. So the police might ask, *Why did you kill Polonius? Where were you when Ophelia drowned?*

2 Work in pairs. List as many questions as possible that the police would ask the same character as in 1 and different characters from other stories. Include as many wh- questions as you can, but ask other questions as well.

3 Work as a class. Say your questions to the class.

4 Kids!

Question tags

1 Work in pairs, A and B. Read this dialogue silently first and then read it aloud in pairs, when you understand it.
A: I don't like kids, do you?
B: Well, they should be seen and not heard, shouldn't they?
A: That's right. *My* kids are all right, aren't they?
B: Oh yes! *Your* kids are, er . . .
A: Well-behaved. Aren't they?
B: Oh yes! Absolutely. Very well-behaved.

2 Work in pairs, A and B.
Person A: Read Activity note 30 on page 144.
Person B: Read Activity note 64 on page 158.

D Accuracy practice

1 Write yes/no or wh- questions.

1 you/go/to Paris/last year?
2 where/be/Tom/today?
3 where/Tom/live/at the moment?
4 Dean/got/any money/these days?
5 your friends/drive/here/today?
6 what/be/the dialling code/for Oxford from London?
7 which/cases/be/Leo's/and who/the others/belong to?

2 Make questions. Put in *are, do, does* or *did* in the right places.

1 How long/it/take/to get/to London by train?
2 Why/you/laughing/and/who/you/laughing at?
3 When/you/buy/that/jacket? It suits you.
4 Which instruments/you/play/nowadays?
5 Where/be/the/plates/and/why/you/not/keep/them in the kitchen?

3 Change these statements into wh- questions.

1 Sheila put that on my desk. (Use *Who*)
2 James left his umbrella on the bus. (Use *Where*)
3 That is the Pickard family's luggage. (Use *Whose*)
4 She means this one. (Use *Which*)
5 They had to drive fifty kilometres before they got to the camp site. (Use *How far*)
6 Snow made all the trains late. (Use *What*)

4 Make indirect questions from the direct questions in brackets.

1 (What qualifications does he need?) Could you tell me ____ ?
2 (What time did John leave?) Can you remember ____ ?
3 (When is Sally coming?) Do you know ____ ?
4 (How much does it cost to rent a flat here?) I wonder ____
5 (Where can I change this money?) I was wondering ____
6 (How long has Phil been living here?) Have you any idea ____ ?
7 (Are Peter and Jean going to be late?) Do you think ____ ?
8 (What time do the shops open in the morning?) I'd like to know ____

5 You want the person you are talking to to agree with these sentences. Add question tags.

1 That programme was really great, ____ ?
2 He can't be a doctor, ____ ?
3 We must get a move on, ____ ?
4 She's living in Spain now, ____ ?
5 You didn't get the answer to that question right, ____ ?
6 You are coming, ____ ?
7 You haven't got a car, ____ ?

7

Present perfect and past simple

A Starting activities

1 Drawing time lines

Present perfect and past simple

Work on your own. Here are time lines for sentences in the present perfect and past simple. The lines represent the period of time the speaker is thinking about ('the past until now' or 'the past').

Present perfect (the past until now)

PAST NOW

I have worked at Star Electronics for two years. (I **like** my job there.)

Past simple (the past)

PAST NOW

I studied maths and science at school. (I **liked** those subjects.)

Choose which of the two time lines is correct for each sentence and draw it:

1. We've lived in London for ten years.
2. James left Africa in 1988.
3. Tracy has never been to Rome.
4. Sophie has made four films in her career so far.
5. Julie made four films in the 1980s.

When you have finished, look at Activity note 9 on page 138.

2 Talking about yourself

Present perfect and past simple

1. Work on your own. Write as many sentences as you can about yourself and your life using the present perfect and the past simple, like this: *I've taught English for twenty-one years. I lived in Germany from 1977 to 1979.*
2. Work in pairs. You want to talk about yourself and so does your partner. If your partner talks for more than a minute or so, interrupt and get the subject back to you and your life as quickly as possible, like this:

   A: *I have always been interested in stamps. I have collected them since I was . . .*

   B: (interrupting) *Really? I have never collected stamps, but a few years ago I started to buy rock and roll records. I . . .*
3. Write down some of your partner's sentences and draw time lines for them.

3 What's happened here?

Present perfect for the present result of a past action

Work in pairs. Look at the pictures and say three or four sentences about what has happened in each of them. Use the present perfect. Examples: *Someone has left a fire burning.* (Picture 1) *Someone has read all her letters.* (Picture 2)

B Grammar guide

1 Present perfect

- We use the PRESENT perfect whenever we talk about the past until NOW.
Use the present perfect for:

a situations that have gone on until now:
I have lived here for the past twenty-five years. (OR *I've lived . . .*)

b repeated actions that have gone on until now:
He has written four books. (OR *He's written . . .*) (He may write more books.)

- *Never, ever, yet* and *before* are usually used with the present perfect to talk about the past until now. *Never* describes an action that has not happened until now.
I've never read 'War and Peace'.
Ever is used to ask whether something has happened until now or not.
Have you ever been to Africa?
Yet is used to say that something has not happened until now (negative statement) or to ask whether it has happened until now (question).
I haven't finished my homework yet.
Have you finished your homework yet?
Before with the present perfect can mean 'until now'.
I've never been in love before.

- We use the PRESENT perfect when we talk about the present result (the result NOW) of past actions.
The children have eaten all the dinner so there is no food left for us now.
NOTE *Already* and *just* are usually used with the present perfect to talk about the present result of a past action.
Already is used in positive statements.
I've already explained, so you don't have to say anything.
Just is often used to talk about a very recent past action.
Jamie has just come in. Let's tell him what's happened.

2 Past simple

We use the past simple whenever we talk about a past, finished situation or action (not the present result of it). Use the past simple to talk about:

a a single past, finished action or situation:
The children ate all the dinner. They ate the meat, the spaghetti and all the cheese.
(They ate the food in the past.)
When I was five we lived in London.

b repeated, finished actions or situations in the past:
When she was young she went to France on holiday every year.
When I was a child we lived in a lot of different countries.
NOTE *When, ago, yesterday* and *last week* are usually used with the past simple.
I saw him when I went to Rome.
He died three years ago.

3 Present perfect and past simple

We often use the present perfect to 'give the news' and then add more information in the past simple.
The children have eaten all the dinner, so there is no food left for us. They ate the meat, the vegetables and all the cheese.

C Activities

1 How healthy is this class?

Present perfect and past simple

You are going to write part of a questionnaire to find out how healthy the class is.

1 Work in pairs or groups. Choose one of the three subjects below. Write seven present perfect and three past simple questions on your subject. Start the questions with: *How much . . .? How many . . .? Have you ever . . .? When did you last . . .? Which of these . . .?*
Examples: *Have you ever stayed up all night? How much fried food did you eat last week?*

Subjects

a Food (Find out if the class has healthy eating habits.)
b Sleep and exercise (Find out if the class gets enough sleep and exercise.)
c General behaviour (Find out if the class has eaten, drunk or done anything that could harm their health.)

2 Ask another pair or group your questions and answer the questions on their questionnaire.

3 Give a report to the whole class about what you found out from your questionnaire. Make a note of any interesting present perfect and simple past sentences that people in the class say.

2 This is your life

Present perfect and past simple

This is your life is a television programme. A well-known person is surprised every week and taken to a party. Guests are introduced from the person's past. Each guest tells an anecdote (an interesting story) about themselves and the famous person when they knew her/him as a child or at school or in early life, or as a colleague, relative, neighbour or friend.
As a class, choose a well-known person and in pairs or groups plan and tell a different anecdote about you and the famous person. The anecdotes should cover different stages of the famous person's life (childhood, youth, early fame etc.). The anecdotes must include some present perfect and past simple verbs. List the verbs that you have used.
Examples: *He has always been a good friend to me. She has always tried to . . . He has always been able to . . . I met her when . . .*

3 Looking after Harry

Present perfect and past simple, questions and short answers

Work in pairs, A and B. A has been out for the day (where?) and has had to leave his or her ten-year-old son Harry with B. Harry has spent time at home with B, but B has also taken Harry out somewhere. Before you read your Activity note, decide together where B has taken Harry. Choose one or two of these:
to a fashion show
fishing
to a boxing match
to the cinema
to play in the park
out with a picnic lunch

Person A: Read Activity note 8 on page 138.
Person B: Read Activity note 47 on page 152.

D Accuracy practice

1 Write sentences. Use the present perfect.

1 Please come on time, Mick. This is the second time/you/be/late this week.
2 /you/ever/try/Richard's home-made cakes? Help yourself!
3 How many countries/you/live/in?
4 I/already/tell/you/the answer. Why are you asking me again?
5 I'm surprised that this car/never/break down/before. It's very old.

2 Choose verbs from the list to complete the sentences. Use the past simple.

have, take (×2), *make, do, get up, teach, stay, eat, dance*

An old woman is talking about the things she did when she was young.

1 When I was young I ____ medicine every winter because I always ____ a terrible cough.
2 When I was young we ____ far bigger meals than people do today.
3 When I was young we ____ the bus to the nearest village every weekend and ____ with the young men.
4 When I was young we never ____ in bed all morning like they do today. We ____ early and ____ all the housework before nine o'clock.
5 When I was young I ____ all my own clothes and I ____ my younger brothers and sisters how to do it too.

3 Use the verbs in the list to complete the sentences. Use the past simple or the present perfect.

leave (×3), *lose* (×2), *fly* (×2), *have, take, eat* (×2)

1 I ____ never ____ from London to Dublin before.
2 We ____ from London Airport to Dublin yesterday. The flight only ____ two hours.
3 ____ you ____ anything yet or shall I make you a sandwich?
4 ____ you ____ anything at the café yesterday or ____ you only ____ a coffee?
5 You won't believe this. Charles ____ Paula! They are getting divorced.
6 Chris ____ Pamela in 1990, but they are still friends.
7 I ____ my wallet! I must have left it on the bus.
8 I ____ my wallet on holiday last year. I ____ it on a bus.

4 Past simple or present perfect in context. Put in the right form of the verb in brackets.

Julie, Sandra and Tom are all students together.

JULIE [1] ____ (you/see) Tom last night?
SANDRA No, but I [2] ____ (just/come) from his house. He's in bed. He [3] ____ (be) very ill in bed for the last three days, actually.
JULIE I'm sorry to hear that. So that's why he [4] ____ (not/go) to the dance last night?
SANDRA Yes. The doctor [5] ____ (see) him twice now. He's coming again tomorrow. Oh, by the way, Tom [6] ____ (send) his love to you when I [7] ____ (see) him.

8

Obligation (*must*), prohibition (*mustn't*) and commands

A Starting activities

1 You've got to take a test

Obligation and prohibition with *have to* and *mustn't*

Work as a class. There is a new learner in your class. Tell the new learner what to do and what not to do. Make sentences with *have to* and *mustn't*.
Examples: *You have to work hard. You mustn't speak your own language during the pairwork.*

2 The Spencer family (Part 1)

Obligation and prohibition with *must*, *mustn't* and the negative imperative

Work in pairs. Mr and Mrs Spencer have a son, Terry, aged twelve and a daughter, Tracy, aged fifteen. They have a lot of problems with both of their children, who never do what their parents want them to. Say sentences that the Spencers could say to their children. Use *must*, *mustn't*, and the negative imperative.
Examples: *Don't try to start the car. You mustn't use my make-up.*

3 The Spencer family (Part 2)

Obligation and prohibition with *ought to* and *ought not to*

Work in pairs. Terry (aged twelve) and Tracy (aged fifteen) are having a lot of problems with Mr and Mrs Spencer, their parents. Terry and Tracy often remind Mr and Mrs Spencer of their duties as parents. Say sentences with *ought to* and *ought not to* that Terry and Tracy could say to their parents.
Examples: *You ought to give me more pocket money. You ought not to stop me wearing fashionable clothes.*

B Grammar guide

1 Obligation

- Use *must*, followed by the infinitive without *to*, for present or future obligation only. There is no past form of *must*. Instead, we use *had to* for the past.
- Use *must* when you have the authority yourself.
  You must go to your room. (Because I say so.)
  I must give up smoking. (It's too expensive for me.)
- Use *have to* or *have got to* when someone else has the authority.
  You have to go to your room. (I heard your mother tell you to.)
  I have got to give up smoking. (My doctor told me to.)
  You can use *must* here but *have got to* is more usual.
- Use *have to* (NOT ~~*have got to*~~) for repeated, general obligation, especially with a one-word adverb of frequency like *often* or *sometimes*.
  I have to catch the early train to get to work on time.
  I often have to do all the typing myself.
  For obligation on a single occasion *have got to* is used more often than *have to*.
  I can't come. I've got to repair the car.
  Have got to often sounds more informal than *have to*.
- Use *ought to* when the obligation is a duty. (It is the right thing to do.)
  You ought to go and see your grandparents more often.
  NOTE *Ought to* is often used to say that although something is the right thing to do, people are not doing it.
  We ought to drive cars that use less petrol. (But we don't.)
  The negative of *ought to* is *ought not to*.
- *Be supposed to* is usually used when the obligation comes from an arrangement or a regulation. Like *ought to*, it often means that someone is not doing what they should.
  You are supposed to queue over there. (But you aren't.)

2 Prohibition

- Use *mustn't* or the negative imperative (*Don't do it.*) to talk about prohibition.
  You mustn't eat with your mouth full.
  Don't open my briefcase.
- *Be not to* is a strong prohibition (when you have a lot of authority or you are angry).
  You are not to go there again, is that clear?
- Don't use *don't have to* to talk about prohibition. *Don't have to* means that something is not necessary.
  You don't have to have a visa to come to Britain from an EC country. (A visa is not necessary.)
  You don't have to come with us. (You can come, but only if you want to.)

3 Commands

- Use the positive imperative for commands.
  Come here!
- *Be + to* can be used for strong commands (when you have a lot of authority).
  You are to be back here by three o'clock.

C Activities

1 A visitor from Mars

Obligation and prohibition with *must, have to* and *mustn't*

1 Work in pairs. Suppose an alien from another planet has landed on earth and is living with you. Imagine the alien following you around to learn about life on earth and doing everything that you do. Explain the 'rules' in your daily life to the alien. Say as many obligation and prohibition sentences as you can.
Examples: *You have to pay to go on a bus. You mustn't put your shoes on before your socks.*

2 Work as a class. Think of your daily routine. Take turns to tell the alien something about a typical day in your life, including as many of your obligation and prohibition sentences as you realistically can.
Examples: *Every morning I have a shower. You must turn the shower off after you have used it. I have bread and butter for breakfast. You mustn't put the butter on the bread with your fingers.*

2 A plan for the environment

Obligation and prohibition

1 Work as a class. Suggest five or six areas where we ought to improve our environment. Think of things like the threat to the ozone layer, air and water pollution, and threats to animals. Make sentences with *must* and *ought to*, like this: *We must stop using cars so much. I think we ought to do something about the destruction of the rain forests.*

2 Work in pairs or groups. Choose one or two of the areas you suggested. Discuss the areas and come up with some ideas for improvements using as many sentences with *must, must not, have to, have got to, ought to* and *ought not to* as you can.
Examples: *Let's stop making cars and then people will have to go to work by bus. We've got to find ways of using plastic to make furniture so that we use less wood.*

3 The desert island: laws of living together

Obligation, prohibition and commands

1 Work as a class. Your class and your teacher are shipwrecked on a desert island together. Decide together what is on the island (for example, trees, other vegetation, wild animals, a stream) and add the details to the drawing of the island below. Decide what has been saved from the shipwreck (not a boat or a two-way radio!).

2 Work in groups or pairs. Write ten 'laws of living together' using *must, must not* and *have to, be + (not) to* and the negative imperative, like this: *Anyone who kills an animal must share it with the rest of the group. You are not to hide food.*

3 Change groups or pairs and compare your 'laws of living together' with other groups or pairs. Try to agree on the ten best laws.

D Accuracy practice

1 **Complete the sentences. Use *must, have to, had to* or *have got to.***

1. Your staff keep forgetting to lock the office door when they leave at night.
   'You ____ all remember to lock the door when you leave.'
2. You are telling a friend about your expedition to the Antarctic last year.
   'We ____ melt the snow to get drinking water.'
3. In Sally's job a lot of work is done in the evenings.
   'She often ____ stay late at the office.'
4. A small boy is late for school because he keeps catching the nine o'clock bus. His teacher is speaking.
   'In future you ____ catch an earlier bus, is that clear?'
5. You have just been to the doctor.
   'I'm overweight. I ____ give up fried food.'
6. You and a friend want to change some money. You are explaining what to do.
   'We ____ fill in these forms and then queue over there.'

2 **Complete the sentences. Use *ought to, ought not to, be supposed to* or *be not supposed to.***

1. It's your own fault that you were injured. You ____ wear special glasses that protect your eyes when you use that machine.
2. I think Derek really ____ help his mother more. She is nearly eighty.
3. Is this the mail room? I ____ pick up a parcel from here.
4. People ____ drink at all if they are going to drive a car.
5. You ____ take the question paper away with you. You ____ hand it in after the exam.
6. They ____ make so much noise every night when they come out of the youth club.

3 **Write prohibition sentences in these situations. Use the negative imperative (*Don't do it.*) or *must not* (both are possible).**

Example: The boss thinks that the staff at the office keep taking paper without asking her first.
Don't/You must not keep taking paper without asking me first.

1. A doctor thinks her patient is overweight because he eats fried food.
2. A driving instructor thinks that the learner driver she is teaching drove through the town centre too quickly.
3. A tour guide wants a group of tourists to stay on the bus until he has got the tickets.
4. The cooker gets hot when you do the cooking. You are talking to a three-year-old child.

9

Nouns, determiners and pronouns

A Starting activities

1 Have you made any progress?

Uncountable nouns and determiners

1 Work as a class. There are three countable nouns in this list. Which are they? (The rest are all uncountable.)

book
bread
cream
gold
jam
oil
snow
wind
wood
advice
football match
fun
help
happiness
health
information
knowledge
love
progress
weather
work
accommodation
cupboard
English
equipment
furniture
homework
luggage
music
rubbish
traffic

When you have finished, look at Activity note 33 on page 145.

2 Work as a class. Here are some determiners that can go before uncountable nouns: *any, enough, (only a) little, more, most (of the), much, some, no, all (of) the.*
Put each of the determiners above into a different sentence with the noun *homework.*
Example: *Is there any homework?*

3 Work in pairs. Write a two-sentence dialogue. Use one of the uncountable nouns from 1 above and one of the determiners from 2 above in each sentence. Example:
A: *Have you made any progress?*
B: *Yes, we've moved all the furniture.*

2 The police are on the way

Singular and plural nouns

1 Work as a class. Which of the nouns below are followed by a singular verb and which are followed by a plural verb?
Nouns: *police, news, people, politics, clothes, pyjamas, shoes, economics, trousers, glasses, scissors, mathematics, goods, savings, premises*

When you have finished, look at Activity note 39 on page 147.

2 Work in pairs. Write five sentences. Each sentence must include one of the nouns from above and each must be six words long.
Examples: *My glasses are on the table.*
The news is all bad today.

3 Work as a class. List one sentence for each noun that people in the class wrote. Imagine that pairs of the sentences that you list are in the same conversation. Find the shortest way of linking the two sentences so they make sense together. Example: *My glasses are on the table. No, on second thoughts don't pass them to me. I won't read the paper after all because the news is all bad today.*

3 Everybody needs somebody to love

Indefinite pronouns

Work in pairs. Make up eight song titles, one for each of the indefinite pronouns in the list below, like this: *Something tells me you're the one for me.*
Indefinite pronouns: *anybody* (or *anyone*), *anything, everybody* (or *everyone*), *everything, nobody* (or *no one*), *nothing, somebody* (or *someone*), *something*

B Grammar guide

1 Uncountable nouns and determiners

- Uncountable nouns always take a singular verb and have no plural form. We do not use *a/an* before an uncountable noun.
  Love is blind. *We are making good progress.* (NOT ~~a good progress~~)
  Many uncountable nouns have a general meaning and also a specific meaning. We can use *the* in the specific meaning.
  Cream is fattening. (All cream, general)
  The cream on that cake looks nice. (That cream, specific)
  We can also use expressions like *a bit of* (which is informal), *a piece of, a loaf/slice of* (bread), *a lump of* (sugar) before uncountable nouns.
  That's a lot to pay for a loaf of bread.
- Here are some common uncountable nouns.
  Substances: *bread, chocolate, cheese, coffee, cream, gold, hair, jam, oil, paper, snow, wind, wood.*
  Abstract nouns: *advice, experience, fun, help, happiness, health, information, knowledge, love, progress, weather, work.*
  Nouns that are uncountable in English but are often countable in other languages: *accommodation, English, music, equipment, furniture, homework, luggage, rubbish, traffic.*
- These determiners are used before uncountable nouns: *any, enough, (only a) little, more, most (of the), a lot of (the), much, some, all (of) the.*
  We use *much* in questions and negative sentences and *a lot of* in positive sentences.
  Have you got much homework to do?
  There isn't much cheese left.
  You need a lot of equipment to go mountain climbing.
  We use *some* in positive sentences and in questions when we want the answer *yes*. We use *any* (to talk about quantity) in other questions and in negative sentences.
  There's some lemonade in the fridge.
  Would you like some of my home-made cake?
  Is there any milk in the fridge?
  The passport office didn't give us any information at all.
  NOTE We can use *no* with a positive verb.
  We have no food left. (= We don't have any food left.)

2 Singular and plural nouns

- These nouns are plural, so use a plural verb with them: *clothes, police.* So are clothes with two parts like *pyjamas, pants, trousers,* things with two parts such as *scissors, glasses, scales* and some words ending in *s*, for example, *goods, premises, savings, outskirts, grounds.*
- These nouns ending in *s* are singular and take a singular verb: *mathematics, politics, economics, news.*

3 Indefinite pronouns

Indefinite pronouns like *anybody* (or *anyone*), *anything, everybody* (or *everyone*), *everything, nobody* (or *no one*), *nothing, somebody* (or *someone*) and *something* are followed by a singular verb.
Everyone we know has a television.

C Activities

1 History never repeats itself

Uncountable nouns

1 Work in pairs or groups. Choose some of the words below and think of or make up proverbs, sayings or slogans using them, like this:
History never repeats itself. All you need is love. Justice for the poor.
Words: *age, anger, childhood, courage, death, education, evil, experience, failure, fashion, freedom, happiness, health, history, justice, loneliness, love, luck, music, power, truth, violence, work, youth*

2 Work as a class. Make a list of all the proverbs, sayings or slogans that people in the class have thought of or made up.

3 Work in pairs or groups. Plan a strip cartoon to illustrate one of the proverbs, sayings or slogans. Your strip cartoon can have from four to six drawings. Each drawing must have a caption below it and can include speech bubbles where the characters speak to each other. When you have finished, show your cartoon to other pairs or groups and see if they can guess which proverb, saying or slogan your cartoon is about.

2 The smallest country in the world

Singular and plural nouns

1 Work as a class. Imagine that the smallest country in the world is an island. It is a very pleasant, perhaps an ideal, place. Agree on a name for the country and decide on these things:

Population of the country
Population of the capital

Capital city (name)	Main natural resources
Unit of currency	Main industries
Agriculture	Newspapers (names)
Main exports	Flag

2 Work in pairs or groups. Describe the country using the nouns below as naturally as possible. Talk about these things: the economy of the country, the political system, the education system, the police, the main problems facing the country at the moment, the country's relations with your country (tourism, state visits, loans etc.).
Nouns: *arms, headquarters, handcuffs, people, police, talks, troops, goods, premises, savings, outskirts, grounds, clothes* (uniform), *trousers, politics, economics*

3 Everyone I meet asks for my autograph

Indefinite pronouns

1 Work in pairs. Imagine that you are one of the people below. As far as possible, each pair should choose a different person so that all four people (a–d) are chosen.

People

a The most famous professional sportsperson in the world. (Who?)
b A person who leads or led a very good life (like Mother Theresa).
c A person who is under a lot of stress (perhaps a business person or a politician).
d A homeless person who sleeps on the streets.

Make sentences about your life using one of the indefinite pronouns in each sentence.
Example: *Everyone I meet asks for my autograph.*

Indefinite pronouns: *anybody, anyone, anything, everybody, everyone, everything, nobody, no one, nothing, somebody, someone, something*

2 Work as a class. Say your sentences to the class. List some sentences about the people whose lives you did not talk about.

3 Work as a class. Choose one of the four people and describe a day in his or her life using as many of your sentences as you realistically can.

D Accuracy practice

1 Which of these are WRONG? There is sometimes more than one which is WRONG.

1 Let me give you (a) **a piece of advice.** (b) **some advice.** (c) **some advices.**
2 Do you want (a) **a piece of bread?** (b) **some bread?** (c) **breads?**
3 I have (a) **homeworks** (b) **some homeworks** (c) **some homework** for you.
4 Can I have (a) **some** (b) **any** chocolate, please?
5 He has (a) **not** (b) **no** experience of this kind of work.
6 You need (a) **much** (b) **a lot of** sugar to make this cake.
7 Would you like two lumps of (a) **sugars?** (b) **sugar?**
8 There's (a) **any** (b) **much** (c) **a lot of** (d) **no** paper for the photocopier. We'll have to get some more.
9 I got (a) **an** (b) **some** (c) **much** information about France from the tourist office.
10 He doesn't have (a) **some** (b) **much** (c) **an** experience of working in an office.

2 Put in the nouns and the correct form of the verbs (singular or plural) in the present simple to complete the sentences.

Nouns: *politics, goods, clothes, news, glasses, scissors, police*
Verbs: *arrive, spend, be* (×2), *have, need, not have to*

1 All the ____ on television ____ bad again.
2 Just how many ____ ____ she got?
3 These ____ ____ sharpening.
4 If ____ ____ damaged they can be replaced.
5 ____ ____ be left to politicians
6 The ____ ____ a lot of time trying to prevent crime.
7 My ____ ____ on the table in that red glasses case.

3 Put in the correct indefinite pronouns to complete the sentences.

anybody (or *anyone*) (×3), *anything, everybody* (or *everyone*), *everything, nobody* (or *no one*), *nothing*

1 Little Ronnie has disappeared. ____ knows where he is.
2 Has ____ seen Aunt Harriet since dinner time?
3 ____ says he won't come back here but I think he will.
4 ____ I tell him seems to make any difference. He won't take advice from ____.
5 You were all here when the accident happened. Didn't ____ notice ____?
6 Come in. ____ is a bit untidy I'm afraid. Sorry.

10

Present perfect (*he has worked*) and present perfect progressive (*he has been working*)

A Starting activities

1 We have been working

Present perfect progressive for actions in progress

Work in pairs. You are both repairing an old house. The work is not finished. Explain to a friend what you have been doing. Use the picture to give you ideas. Use the present perfect progressive, like this: *We have been repairing the roof.*

2 What have you done?

Present perfect for completed actions

Work in the same pairs. You have finished all the work on the house. Explain what you have done. Use the present perfect, like this: *We have repaired the roof.*

3 Choose the rule

Present perfect and present perfect progressive

Work as a class. Look at the sentences below. Notice how the present perfect is correct in 1a and the present perfect progressive is correct in 2a.

1 a I can go home now. *I've typed all my boss's letters.* ✓
  b I can go home now. *I've been typing all my boss's letters.* ×
2 a You look tired. *Have you been shopping?* ✓
  b You look tired. *Have you shopped?* ×

All the rules below are correct, but choose the ones which explain why 1b and 2b are wrong.

(i) Use the present perfect and not the present perfect progressive to talk about completed actions.
(ii) Use the present perfect to talk about naturally short actions.
(iii) Use the present perfect progressive for temporary actions or situations.
(iv) Use the present perfect progressive to describe actions in the recent past that you think have been happening because of something you can see now (present evidence).

When you have finished, look at Activity note 48 on page 152.

B Grammar guide

1 Present perfect

We use the present perfect and not the present perfect progressive when we want to make it clear that an action has been completed.
We have repaired the fridge. (The fridge works now.)

- We usually use the present perfect and not the present perfect progressive with state verbs: *be, seem, prefer, believe, know, like, love, hate.*
  How long have you known John? (NOT ~~*been knowing*~~)
- We use the present perfect and not the present perfect progressive for naturally short actions like *break, fall (over), start.*
  Have you broken the window? (NOT ~~*been breaking*~~)
- We use the present perfect and not the present perfect progressive with *ever, never* and *yet.*
  I haven't told her yet. (NOT ~~*been telling*~~) *I have never met Tony.*

2 Present perfect progressive

We use the present perfect PROGRESSive when we want to emphasize an action or situation in PROGRESS and not its completion. *We've been repairing the fridge.* (It may or may not work now.) We use the present perfect progressive for:

- temporary actions and situations:
  I've been using Joanna's car while I've been staying with her. (NOT ~~*have used*~~ and ~~*have stayed*~~)
- actions in the recent past that we think have been happening because of something we can see now (present evidence):
  Your eyes are red. You've been crying. (NOT ~~*have cried*~~)
  (This is often used to complain. *Hey! Somebody has been drinking my coffee!*)
- talking about how long something has been going on:
  How long have you been learning English?
  He has been writing to her for ten years.
- The present perfect progressive is more commonly used in informal speech.

3 Present perfect or present perfect progressive

- You can use the present perfect progressive with these state verbs, if you want to emphasize a situation in progress and not its completion: *see, hear, look, taste, smell, want, realize, remember.*
  I've been hearing funny noises.
  He's been looking miserable since his dog died.
  I've been wanting one of those new computers for ages.
  If you do not wish to emphasize the progressive nature of the situation, you can use the present perfect simple with these verbs.
  I've heard a lot of funny noises lately.
  That house has looked a mess for years.
  I've always wanted one of those.
- Some verbs suggest an action in progress by their meaning and these can be used both with the present perfect and the present perfect progressive, with little difference in meaning: *live, rain, sit, study, wait, work.*
  It's been raining for hours. *It's rained non-stop for hours.*
  I have worked/have been working at the bank for three years.

C Activities

1 Quiz contestants

Present perfect progressive for how long something has been going on

1 Work with a partner. You are going to take turns to be the host of a television quiz show. Working together, plan or write introductions for both of you. Use present perfect progressive sentences to say things like where your partner has been living, where he or she has been working (or studying) and what interesting things he or she has been doing lately.
Example: *This is Jean. She has been working as a cleaner for the last three weeks.*

2 Work as a class. Introduce each other to the class as television quiz contestants.

2 A new plan for the club

Present perfect progressive

1 Work in pairs, A and B. You and your partner have just taken over a youth club for twelve to eighteen year-olds. There have been problems with the club. You and your partner are going to work together to solve some of the problems.
Person A: Read Activity note 10 on page 138.
Person B: Read Activity note 49 on page 152.

2 Work as a class. Tell the class about any problems not in the Activity notes and your solutions to all the problems. Add the problems that other people say to your list.

3 The TV news

Present perfect and present perfect progressive

1 Work as a class. Plan a television news programme, with five or six items of news in it. Use the present perfect for finished events and the present perfect progressive for events which are still going on. You can use real events or make them up. Use the ideas below to help you.

Ideas
statesman's visit to . . .
forest fire in . . .
plane crash in . . .
tennis match between . . .
new film about . . .
inflation (up/down)
royal baby
fighting in . . .
. . . met the president of . . .
a new television series about . . .
prison riot at . . .

Examples: *There has been a prison riot at the new prison and several prisoners have climbed onto the roof. . . Stephen Spielberg has been making a new film about . . .*

2 Work as a class. Five or six people in the class say one item each of the television news programme. Help anybody who needs help with his or her item. List sentences from the news with the present perfect or present perfect progressive.

D Accuracy practice

1 Present perfect or present perfect progressive? Choose the correct one, (a) or (b).

1 (a) I have been painting / (b) I have painted } the kitchen. I should be finished soon.

2 (a) You have been breaking / (b) You have broken } my window!

3 (a) I've liked / (b) I've been liking } the Beatles since I was twelve.

4 Oh no! Karen has just { (a) been falling over. / (b) fallen over.

5 (a) Somebody has read / (b) Somebody has been reading } my letters. This one has been opened.

6 (a) It has been snowing / (b) It has snowed } here for days. It won't stop until next week.

2 Put the state verbs in brackets into the present perfect (*I have remembered*) or the present perfect progressive (*I have been remembering*).

1 Happy birthday, darling. I (remember) to buy you a present.
2 Lately, I (remember) the happy times we spent together all those years ago.
3 She (prefer) classical music to pop ever since she was a child.
4 Surely Andrew (believe) in fairies for long enough. Let's tell him the truth.
5 Arthur (taste) all the food as I put it on the table.

3 Write sentences. Use the present perfect or the present perfect progressive or both. Write two sentences where possible.

The information is from a child's school report.

1 He/not do/enough work
2 He/start/this new subject well
3 He/make/a bit more effort this term
4 He/not learn/to behave properly in class yet
5 He/never like/maths, and he/do/very little work all term

4 Present perfect and present perfect progressive in context. Put in the right form of the verb in brackets. Sometimes more than one answer is possible.

This is a job reference in formal English.

William Empson [1] ____ (work) in the Parks Department for the last six months. Throughout this time he [2] ____ (train) as a gardener under my supervision and I can confirm that I [3] ____ (watch) his progress closely. I must inform you that Mr Empson [4] ____ (be) in prison for burglary. However, during his time with us he [5] ____ (be) in charge of money several times and [6] ____ (never/attempt) to steal it. For most of his time here he [7] ____ (help) to grow new trees in the greenhouses. He [8] ____ (learn) quickly and he [9] ____ (not/be) late for work once. We would recommend Mr Empson for the post he [10] ____ (apply) for.

11

Permission and requests: *can, could, may, be allowed to, will, would*

A Starting activities

1 Can I use your phone, please?

Asking for permission using *can, could* and *may*

1. Work in pairs. You are both guests at someone else's home. Use *may* (formal), *could* (less formal) or *can* (informal) to ask for permission to do a different thing at all of these people's homes:
   your grandparents' (or uncle and aunt's) home
   a close friend's home
   the boss's home
   your teacher's home
   a neighbour's home

   Examples: *Can I use your phone, please?* (at a close friend's home)
   May I have a look at this book? (at the boss's home)
2. Say your sentences to the class. Write down good examples of formal requests (using *may*), less formal requests (using *could*) and informal requests (using *can*) that people in the class say.

2 Will you help with the washing up, please?

Requests using *can, could, will* or *would*

Work with a partner. Decide which of the things in the list of requests you would ask a guest at your home to do for you and take it in turns to make requests. Use *can you* or *will you.* If you need to be more polite, because the request is more unusual, use *could you* or *would you* and give a reason for the request, like this: *Would you answer the phone, please? I'm just feeding the baby.*

Requests
move a chair
do the washing up
clean the floor
read to small children
make coffee
open a window
open a bottle that you can't open
do some gardening
change a baby's nappy
drive someone to the station
feed the cat
move a cupboard from one room to another
take the rubbish out to the dustbin
pass something on the table to you
answer the phone
put a cassette on
lend you some money

3 Sorting them out

Permission and requests

Work in pairs or as a class. Say whether these sentences asking for permission and making requests are formal or informal.

1. Would you mind not smoking, please?
2. Can my friend come too?
3. May I ask you a question about the salary for this job?
4. Can you put it down over there, please?
5. Mr Jackson, would you tell the staff that there is a meeting in room 204 at four o'clock, please?

When you have finished, look at Activity note 53 on page 153.

B Grammar guide

1 Permission

- In informal situations, speaking to friends or people you know well, use *can I* or *can we* to ask for permission (to ask if you can do something).
  Can I use your phone?
  You can use *could I/we* in more formal situations or when you are not sure you will get the permission you are asking for.
  Could I ask you a personal question?
  May is even more formal than *can*. Use it when you are even less sure of getting permission or when you think that what you are asking could be unwelcome.
  Mr President, may I ask you what you plan to do about the economy?
  We can also use *would you mind if* to ask for permission.
  Would you mind if I invited a few friends round?
- Use *can* or *may* but not *could* to give permission.
  Yes, you can/may.
- To talk about something which is permitted now, use *can* or *is/are allowed to.* If it is not permitted, use *can't* or *isn't/aren't allowed to.*
  You can come and go as you please.
  You are allowed to go in if you are over twenty-one.
  You can't go in there at the moment.
  You aren't allowed to go in there if you are under twenty-one.
- If something was permitted in the past use *could* or *was/were allowed to.*
  When we were fifteen we could stay out until midnight.
  When I was fifteen I was allowed to have parties at home without my parents.

2 Requests

- Use *can you* or *could you* (but not *may*) to make requests (to ask someone to do something). *Can* is informal, *could* is more formal or polite.
  Can you let John through, please?
  Could you help me wash the car, Jean?
  You can use *can, could* or *may* with *I* or sometimes *we* (e.g. *can I*) in requests when you are asking someone to give you something.
  May I have a cup of coffee?
  In this last example, you are requesting someone to get you a cup of coffee, which is why it is a request and not a sentence asking for permission.
- Use *will you* to make requests when you don't have to be particularly polite.
  Will you let the cat out, please?
- Use *would you* or *would you mind* when you want to be more polite or formal.
  Would you make the arrangements, please?
  Would you mind is followed by the *-ing* form.
  Would you mind telling Peter the bad news when he comes in?

C Activities

1 They told us we were too young

Talking about permission

1 Work with a partner. Say what you were allowed to do or weren't allowed to do at every age between three and fourteen, like this: *I was allowed to stay up until midnight when I was ten. I wasn't allowed to cross the road on my own until I was eight.*

Ideas

ride a bicycle on the road
go out on your own
go on holiday on your own
go out alone with boys/girls
have parties at home when your parents were out
drink wine

2 As a class, compare your sentences. Who was allowed to go out with boys/girls at the youngest age? Who was allowed to go on holiday without their parents at the earliest age?

2 Well, just a few friends perhaps

Asking for permission and making requests

Work in pairs, A and B. Decide who is A and who is B. A is fifteen and is looking after the family home for the first time while her or his parents are away for the weekend. B is one of A's parents.

Person A: Read Activity note 16 on page 140.
Person B: Read Activity note 54 on page 154.

3 The happy day

Requests

1 Work in pairs, A and B, or groups of four, pair A and pair B. Your child is getting married. A (or pair A) is the parent or parents of the bride and B (or pair B) is the parent or parents of the groom. Make requests to each other about the arrangements for the wedding reception, like this: *Would you mind finding a band for us? Could we choose the flowers?*

Ideas

Place (bride's home/groom's home/hired hall/hotel)
Food and drink (buffet/meal/home-made/from a caterer/cake)
Music (a band/a group/guests' own entertainment/a disco)
Seating arrangements
Date and time

2 Work as a class. Tell the class who agreed to do what for the wedding and the class will say if you have forgotten anything. If you have, you may need to make some more requests.

D Accuracy practice

1 Ask for permission or make a request using *can, could* or *may*. More than one answer is often possible.

1. You want to write down your friend's telephone number but you haven't got a pen. Your friend has got one which you want to borrow.
2. You are at a business meeting and someone is speaking. You have a question to ask. You say 'Excuse me . . .'
3. You want to change a five-pound note to make a telephone call. You stop a person in the street.
4. A waitress is offering you cakes. You want the chocolate one with the cream on top.
5. Your father is handing round biscuits at a party. You would like one.
6. You want to go to a higher level English class. You ask the teacher.
7. You are having dinner with people you do not know very well. You want another cup of coffee.
8. You are on a train and someone has finished reading their newspaper. You want to read it.

2 Fay is ill in bed and has to ask her friend to do things for her. What does she say? Use *can, could, will* or *would*. More than one answer is often possible.

1. Fay wants her book, which is on the other side of the room. She asks her friend to pass it to her.
2. Fay wants some chicken soup for dinner.
3. Fay wants her friend to stop smoking.
4. Fay doesn't want people to bring her any more fruit.
5. Fay wants some magazines to read. She asks her friend to get her some.

3 Permission and requests in context. Put in *would* or *may*. This is formal, spoken English.

A meeting of the sales and marketing staff of Britforce PLC

MRS PEERS Right. [1]____ you look at the sales figures for last year which are in front of you? I think you all have them.

MR ROGERS Excuse me, [2]____ I ask something about the figures for Japan?

MRS PEERS Yes, you [3]____ . What do you want to know?

MR ROGERS Do they include sales for South Korea when it was still under the Japan office?

MRS PEERS Yes, they do. And now (she coughs) . . . Oh dear! [4]____ you pass me that water jug, please, and a glass? Thank you. And [5]____ you switch on the light? It's getting a bit dark in here. Thank you. Right. Now [6]____ I ask you about the Far East for next year, Alan? [7]____ you look after our office in China?

MR FRASER Yes, Mrs Peers. Thank you very much.

MRS PEERS That's all right. And [8]____ I ask you, Bill, to continue in the new office in South Korea?

MR ROGERS [9]____ I ask if that will still come under Japan for finance or will I have my own finance staff in Seoul?

MRS PEERS Finance? Oh, that's still under Japan, Bill. Still under Japan.

Articles

A Starting activities

1 I'd like a pair of jeans with a belt

***a/an* and *the* contrasted**

1 Work in pairs. You are buying clothes. Say what you want using *a/an* and adding a brief description using *with*, like this: *I'd like a pair of jeans with a belt.*

2 Work as a class. Make a list of your sentences.

3 Work in pairs. Take turns to complain about everything on the list, using *the*. You can be as angry as you like when you complain. Example: *The pair of jeans I bought is too small.*

2 Are men and women equal?

Zero article with countable nouns

1 Work in pairs. Tell your partner all the ways that men and women are different. Include stereotypes and clichés. (You don't have to agree with everything you say.) Start each sentence with *men* or *women*, like this: *Women cry more. Men are stronger.*

2 Work as a class. List all the differences between men and women that people in the class thought of.

3 Work in pairs or groups. Decide which differences you disagree with and which you agree with. Put them in order, with the one you disagree with most at the top of your list.

3 Paper is made from trees

Zero article with uncountable nouns

1 Work in pairs or groups. Write as many true facts about each of the uncountable nouns as you can. Example: *When snow melts it becomes water.*

Uncountable nouns: *water, gold, paper, snow, oil, wood, rain, sand, meat, salt*

2 Read your sentences to the class. You get a point for every sentence with the facts correct. You lose a point if the facts in your sentence are wrong. Example: *Water freezes at ten degrees centigrade.* (Wrong, lose one point.) The winner is the pair or group with the most points.

B Grammar guide

1 The indefinite article (*a/an*)

- *A/an* is used with singular countable nouns only (*a book, an orange*).
- Before vowels (*a, e, i, o* and *u*) *a* changes to *an* but the change depends on the pronunciation and not just on the spelling. So we say *an hour* (*an* because the *h* is not sounded) but *a uniform* and *a European* (*a* is used before *u* and *eu* when they sound like the *y* in *you*).
- The usual meaning of *a/an* is 'only one and it does not matter which one'.
  I'd like a cup of coffee, please. (= one cup of coffee and any cup of coffee)
- When a singular uncountable noun is mentioned for the first time, use *a/an.*
  Alan took a book off the shelf.
- We can use *some/a lot of/any* with plural countable nouns.
  I've got some nails, but I haven't got any screws.

2 The definite article (*the*)

- *The* is used with singular countable nouns (*the book*), with plural countable nouns (*the books*), and with uncountable nouns (*snow, spaghetti*), in their specific sense (not in their general sense).
  The snow was over a metre deep last winter.
  Other determiners are also possible before uncountable nouns in their specific sense.
  Is there any snow on the motorway, or is it clear?
- The most common meaning of *the* is 'the one you know about' ('a specific and definite one'). In context, we often know about something because it has already been mentioned.
  Alan took a book off the shelf. He opened the book and started to read.

3 Zero article

- There is no article before:
  plural countable nouns in their general sense: *Cats can see in the dark.*
  uncountable nouns in their general sense: *Snow at night is beautiful.*
- There is no article before proper names (*John*) and titles (*Mr*).

4 Phrases with indefinite, definite, or zero article

- The indefinite article is used:
  in exclamations: *What a mess!*
  in descriptions of frequency, speed and cost: *once a day, 30 km an hour*
- The definite article is used:
  when there is only one (or only one which is important to the speaker): *the butcher's, the zoo, the police*
  for nationalities and *the* + adjective: *the British, the blind, the disabled*
  for regions, mountain ranges, oceans and seas: *the Middle East, the Alps*
  for hotels, restaurants, pubs, theatres and cinemas: *The Albion, the Odeon*
- There is no article (zero article):
  for some institutions used for their main purpose (schools, hospitals, churches etc.): *Richard goes to school in the village.* (BUT *The school is opposite our house.*)
  before the names of meals: *Let's have lunch.* (BUT *The lunch was cold.*)
  for continents, countries and cities: *Asia, Italy* (BUT *the UK*), *Athens*
  for mountains and lakes: *Mount Snowdon, Lake Eyre*
  for streets (except *the High Street* and *the Oxford road,* which means 'the road which leads to Oxford'): *West Street, New Road*

C Activities

1 Maggie's restaurant

Indefinite, definite and zero article

1 Work in pairs or groups. Put in any missing articles and make any other changes necessary to make complete sentences.

A note from Helen to Maggie, January 16

> Mr Briggs from restaurant supplies shop phoned. Said he can't deliver fridge and cooker until this afternoon. I've got to go to butcher's. Can you stay in restaurant, let restaurant supplies man in and wait by phone? Have taken booking for Saturday. It's in reservation book.

Some headlines in the local newspaper, January 23

New restaurant opens in Fulchester
Maggie's best new restaurant in town
Food delicious at Maggie's
All that is best in Thai and Malaysian food

A note from Maggie to Helen, February 10

> Can you prepare tomato roses for tonight, please? (Peel ripe firm tomato so skin comes off in one piece. Wind piece of skin round and round then spread petals of tomato rose in palm of your hand.) I will put advertisement in newspaper for waiter/waitress, so please be patient just little bit longer.

An advertisement in the local newspaper, March 5

Waiter/Waitress wanted for Maggie's restaurant. Evenings and Sunday lunchtimes only. Experience of Thai and Malaysian food advantage.

A note from Helen to Maggie, March 5

> This is quick note to say I'm not coming in this evening. Or tomorrow. Maybe never. Sorry. Can't cope with being waitress and cook and doing washing up and all rest of it any more. Have done tomato roses for this evening.

An excerpt from 'The Best Restaurants in Britain Guide'

> *Maggie's Restaurant, Fulchester*
> Unusual small restaurant (six tables) serves Thai and Malaysian food. Book in advance. Food excellent but service poor.

2 Work as a class. Tell the story of Maggie's restaurant in your own words and then write it down, underlining all the indefinite and definite articles and marking all the zero articles.

2 Seventy-five-word stories

The 'rules' for articles

Work in pairs or groups. Write a story that is exactly seventy-five words long (not including the title). Your story must include the following (see the Grammar guide for examples of all of them):

(i) *a* (not *an*) + a word which starts with a vowel
(ii) *an* (not *a*) + a word which does not start with a vowel
(iii) *the* + an uncountable noun in its specific sense
(iv) zero article before a plural countable noun in its general sense

D Accuracy practice

1 Which is correct, (a) or (b)?

1 Julie goes to (a) **church** (b) **the church** every Sunday.
2 Go straight ahead to (a) **church** (b) **the church**, then turn left.
3 I'm a bit upset. Lee's in (a) **hospital.** (b) **the hospital.** He's quite ill.
4 My sister works at (a) **hospital.** (b) **the hospital.** She's a cleaner.
5 In Britain, children go to (a) **school** (b) **the school** from nine o'clock until four o'clock every day.

2 Which is correct, (a) or (b)?

1 My wife is away on business in (a) **Far East.** (b) **the Far East.**
2 It's the biggest theme park in (a) **UK.** (b) **the UK.**
3 The highest mountain in (a) **the Himalayas** (b) **Himalayas** is (a) **Mount Everest.** (b) **the Mount Everest.**
4 They live on a small island in (a) **Pacific.** (b) **the Pacific.**
5 She's travelling in (a) **the Europe** (b) **Europe** and (a) **Middle East.** (b) **the Middle East.**

3 Which is correct, (a) or (b)?

1 (a) **Spaghetti** (b) **The spaghetti** you ate yesterday was for today's dinner.
2 I like (a) **spaghetti.** (b) **the spaghetti.**
3 We often go to the park to look at (a) **flowers.** (b) **the flowers.**
4 (a) **Computer games** (b) **The computer games** are one of the things in the modern world that old Mr Tomkins doesn't like.
5 There's been an accident. Call (a) **police** (b) **the police.**

4 Put in *a/an, some, any* or *a lot of* only where necessary.

1 Peter and Alison haven't got ____ children.
2 ____ children would be ____ problem for them at the moment as they have ____ work to do and they don't have ____ money.
3 Unfortunately they don't have ____ interesting hobbies either. I think one of them should have ____ hobby.
4 Their lives consist entirely of ____ work. ____ people live like that.
5 They aren't even interested in ____ travel. Sad, isn't it?

5 Write this letter again, putting in articles where necessary.

A letter from Doris Winter to the manager of her local bank:

I went to bank yesterday in order to arrange for cashpoint card and credit card but I was told that I had to make written application. My name is Doris Winter and I am German national, staying in United Kingdom for one year to improve my English. I was also asked to provide details of my bank account in Germany. Account is at bank in Hamburg. Enclosed cheque has my account number.
I understand that credit card they provided cannot be used here. You may contact manager (Mr Fuchs) who will provide reference for me if you require one.

13

Past perfect (*he had written*) and past perfect progressive (*he had been writing*)

A Starting activities

1 What happened first?

Past perfect

1 Work in pairs. Write 1 by the action which happened first and 2 by the action which happened after it. Example:
- *The audience left* (2)
- *after the film had finished.* (1)

a – We got married in 1990,
– just a year after we had fallen in love.

b – As soon as I got home, I saw
– that someone had broken into my flat.

c – When he crashed the car,
– he had just drunk four glasses of wine.

d – Unfortunately we arrived at the cinema
– after the film had started.

e – By the time I got home
– they had eaten all the cake.

2 One verb in each of the sentences above is in the past simple. The other verb is in the past perfect. Is the past perfect used for the first action or the action which happened after it?

When you have finished, look at Activity note 11 on page 139.

2 A thing of two halves

Past perfect

1 Work in pairs, A and B. Without showing B, A writes the first half only of five sentences using a verb in the past perfect each time, like this: *As soon as we had finished lunch . . .* Start with: *when, by the time, as soon as, after.* Without looking at what A is writing, B writes the second half of five sentences using past simple verbs, like this: . . . *John stayed at home.*

2 Put the sentence halves together, changing them until they make sense. Example: *As soon as we had finished lunch John went home.*

3 Re-write all five sentences putting B's second halves (with the past simple verbs) first. Example: *John went home as soon as we had finished lunch.*

3 How long?

Past perfect progressive

1 Work in pairs. Does the speaker emphasize the length of the action in sentence (i) or sentence (ii)? Example:

(i) *By the time I got home they had eaten all the cake.*
(ii) *By the time I got home they had been eating for two hours.*

Answer: (ii)

a (i) He had been driving for hours before they caught him.
(ii) They caught him before he had driven very far.

b (i) As soon as they had cleaned the kitchen, they started on the dining room.
(ii) Before they started on the dining room, they had been cleaning the kitchen all morning.

2 Are the sentences where the speaker emphasizes the length of the action in the past perfect or in the past perfect progressive?

When you have finished, look at Activity note 46 on page 151.

B Grammar guide

1 Past perfect

When there are two actions in the past, we use the past perfect for the earlier (first) action. We are looking back from a point in the past to an earlier action.
We got married in 1990, just a year after we had fallen in love.
As soon as I got home I saw that someone had broken into my flat.

- Use the past perfect (not the past perfect progressive) when the action took a very short time (like breaking a window).
  When they saw they had broken the window, they ran away.
  (NOT ~~*had been breaking*~~)
- Use the past perfect (not the past perfect progressive) with some state verbs: *seem, prefer, believe, know, like, suppose.*
  I hadn't known about it at the time. (NOT ~~*hadn't been knowing*~~)

2 Past perfect progressive

Use the past perfect progressive to emphasize how long something took. As with the past perfect, we are looking back from a point in the past to an earlier action.
By the time I got home they had been eating for two hours.
He had been driving for hours before they caught him.

3 Link words

When, after, as soon as, before and *by the time* are often used in past perfect and past perfect progressive sentences.
When Jane had had her turn, I had mine.
After he had been practising for an hour, James could play the tune perfectly.
As soon as Rosie had finished the meal she went home.
George had been queuing for hours before he got his money.
She had been waiting for two hours by the time I got there.
She had waited for two hours by the time the train came.

4 Past perfect or past simple?

- Sometimes we look back from a point in the past to an earlier action but we do not use the past perfect. We use the past simple instead.

a We can use the past simple when the first action was short and was closely followed by the second action.
After I broke the window, I just ran off.
Though even here a past perfect is still possible.
After I had broken the window, I just ran off.

b When it is clear that we are talking about an earlier action, we use the past simple for any other information about the same action.
When I got back after lunch, Jean told me that somebody had phoned when I was out. (~~*had been out*~~ would be wrong in that sentence.)

- Use the past simple when two past actions happened at the same time and there is no earlier (past perfect) action.
  When he saw her, he screamed.

C Activities

1 A good party

Past perfect progressive

Work in pairs. Imagine that the class had a party last week (where?) but something delayed you on your way there (what?). Decide what people in the class had been doing at the party (and for how long) before you arrived. Use the past perfect progressive, like this: *By the time we arrived at the party, Maria had been dancing for two hours.*

2 An insurance claim

Past perfect and past perfect progressive

Work in pairs, A and B. Last year A went on holiday. It was the worst holiday of A's life. A's wife/husband got food poisoning and had to go to hospital. A also had a car crash. And while A was on the beach, having a good time, somebody broke into the hotel room and stole some clothes, a radio and some jewellery. Fortunately, A had taken out holiday insurance. A is now at the insurance office, making an insurance claim. B is the insurance officer.

Person A: Read Activity note 12 on page 139.
Person B: Read Activity note 50 on page 152.

3 The trial of Sammy Banks

Past perfect, past perfect progressive and past simple

Sammy Banks had been playing cards with some friends. The friends say he had been drinking. He then drove home, late at night, which was wrong of him. He had been driving for half an hour when he hit a pedestrian, who had been walking along a narrow country road. Sammy drove on. When a policeman stopped him Sammy said he was going to report the accident when he got home. This is Sammy's trial.

1 Work in pairs (A and B) or in groups of four. In pairs, A is Sammy and B is the lawyer asking questions. In groups of four there is a prosecution and a defence lawyer, both asking questions, Sammy and a judge. The judge controls the activity. Use past perfect, past simple and past perfect progressive questions and answers where you can. Use the ideas below to help you.

Ideas
Exactly how much had Sammy drunk at the card game?
Had Sammy been driving too fast when she/he hit the pedestrian?
Did Sammy stop when she/he hit the pedestrian, or just drive on?
What was the pedestrian wearing? Dark or light clothes?

2 Work as a class. The judges from some of the pairs or groups sum up the trial. Make separate lists of past perfect, past progressive and past simple sentences from the trial.

D Accuracy practice

1 Choose verbs from the list to complete the sentences. Use the past perfect.

die, eat, beat, stop, take

1. I was the one who made the cake and by the time I got home they ____ it all.
2. 'Anne went to Mrs Peters' funeral yesterday.'
   'Oh dear! I didn't even know that Mrs Peters ____.'
3. Charlie beat Fred at tennis for the first time yesterday. He ____ (not) Fred before.
4. I saw Sophie smoking. I was disappointed. She told me she ____ last year.
5. I'm sorry, I didn't know you lent it to Frances. I thought she ____ it from your room.

2 Choose verbs from the list to complete the sentences. Use the past perfect progressive.

smoke, play, visit, read, steal

1. When I went into the room I could smell cigarette smoke. Obviously, somebody ____ in there.
2. As soon as they caught him, he told them everything. He ____ money from the company and using it to pay for his holidays.
3. By the time the match had finished they ____ for two hours.
4. By the time she got better I ____ her in hospital for six months.
5. By the end of May I still hadn't finished the book and I ____ it for six months.

3 Past perfect or past simple? Put in the right form of the verb in brackets.

1. When Sarah got off the bus it was raining heavily; she ____ (go) into a shop to buy a new umbrella because she ____ (leave) her old umbrella at home.
2. He ____ (retire) from work early, but he ____ (work) hard all his life.
3. As soon as he ____ (see) her, he just ____ (laugh).
4. As soon as he ____ (visit) her in hospital and knew she was all right, he ____ (catch) the next bus home.

4 Past perfect or past perfect progressive in context. Put in the correct form of the verb in brackets.

PLAYER My best moment in the match was when I realized the game [1]____ (finish) and I [2]____ (become) a tennis champion. I [3]____ (win)! At that moment I [4]____ (become) the best tennis player in the world.

REPORTER And when you won, how long [5]____ (you/play) tennis?

PLAYER I started just before I finished school. That means I [6]____ (play) for about six years when I won Wimbledon.

REPORTER You [7]____ (beat) some good players before you won that tournament.

PLAYER Yes. Ever since I started as a tennis professional I [8]____ (win) games regularly, until my injury.

REPORTER Yes. What did you do to hurt your shoulder so badly?

PLAYER I [9]____ (not/hit) the ball well for some time, so I practised a lot. Then one day I realized I [10]____ (damage) my shoulder by trying too hard. I had to give up playing tennis because of it.

14

Relative clauses

A Starting activities

1 About relative clauses

Different relative clauses

1 Work as a class. What are the relative clauses in sentences a–g? For example, in the sentence *Tom Dennismore, who is twenty-seven, wrote 'My Life in Pictures'*, the relative clause is *who is twenty-seven.*

a That man who is sitting over there is an old friend of my father's.

b The two cars which are in front of the entrance must be removed immediately, please.

c The person who gave you that information is an idiot.

d The other train that was cancelled was going to London.

e Mrs Stanley, whose parents had once lived in the village, looked quickly at all the pretty houses and decided she liked it there.

f Seven-year-old Roy, who had never been polite, rudely shouted 'Be quiet' as the old man was finishing his story.

2 Only one of these two sentences should have commas round the relative clause. Where should the commas go?

a Arthur Grimes who is thirty painted 'The Cherry Tree'.

b The woman who lived next door was arrested last week.

When you have finished, look at Activity note 40 on page 148.

2 Tokyo, which is . . .

who, which, where, that, whose

1 Work as a class. Think of ten people, places, emotions (for example, 'love') and issues (for example, 'the environment') which interest you. One person in the class chooses one of the people, places, emotions or issues from your list. A second person adds a relative clause beginning with *who, which, that* or *whose* and a third person finishes the sentence in a way that makes sense. Example:
Person 1: *The environment,*
Person 2: *which is very important,*
Person 3: *is something we should all care about.*

2 Work in pairs or groups of three and continue the Activity. If you are working in pairs, A speaks for Person 1 and 3, and B for Person 2 – then change round. Use *who, which, where, that* and *whose.*

3 Off-putting film titles

who, which, where, that, whose

1 Work in pairs or small groups. Most film titles aim to persuade people to see the film. Just for fun, think of some off-putting film titles that would persuade people not to see the film. Each title must contain a relative clause with *who, which, where, that* or *whose.* Here are some ideas for the first words of the titles but use your own ideas if you can.

Ideas: The Exercise Book . . ., A Piece of Cheese . . ., A Small . . ., A Table . . .
Example: *A Small Hole Which I Noticed In My Jacket*

2 Work as a class. Tell the other people in the class your titles and list the best of theirs.

B Grammar guide

1 Relative clauses

Clauses are parts of a sentence that have a main verb. Clauses with a relative pronoun (like *who* or *which*) are called relative clauses. In the sentence *That girl who just came in is in our class* the relative clause is *who just came in.*

2 *who, which, whose, where* and *that*

- *Who* is used for people, *which* is used for things and *whose* can be used for people or things. *Whose* means 'belonging or referring to'. You can use *where* in a relative clause to talk about a place, as in *The town/room/street where . . .*
- *That* can replace *who* or *which* in identifying relative clauses only (see 3 below). *That* is less formal than *who* or *which.*

a *The man who/that she loved so much left without saying goodbye.*
b *That film which/that we went to see last week is on television tomorrow.*
c *South Korea, whose industry is developing quickly, can now produce microchips as cheaply as Japan.*

3 Identifying and non-identifying relative clauses

- In sentence (a) in 2 (above) the relative clause identifies the man. It tells you which man. It is an identifying relative clause. If you take the identifying relative clause away, the sentence will lose a lot of its original meaning. But sentence (c) does not identify South Korea. It gives more information about South Korea, but if you remove it the sentence keeps much of its original meaning. The relative cause in sentence (c) is a non-identifying relative clause.
- Non-identifying relative clauses must have a comma after the noun.
This is Mr Turner, who is a painter.
If the sentence continues after the clause, there is a comma at the end of the clause.
This is Mr Turner, who is a painter, and his wife.
Non-identifying relative clauses are more common in formal spoken English and in written English than in conversational or informal English.

4 Leaving out the relative pronoun: *-ing* and *-ed* clauses

- When the relative pronoun (*who, which* or *that*) is the subject of a clause, it can be replaced by *-ing* (present participle) or *-ed* (past participle) forms.

a *The woman who is sitting on that bench looks ill* (with a relative pronoun) is the same as *The woman sitting on that bench looks ill* (present participle, no relative pronoun). Use an *-ing* form when you want to describe someone's actions now or at a past time.
b *The woman who was injured in the accident was going to work* (with a relative pronoun) is the same as *The woman injured in the accident was going to work* (past participle, no relative pronoun). The *-ed* forms are passive.

- When *who, which* or *that* is the object you can also leave out the relative pronoun. *The woman (who) I loved went away.*

C Activities

1 The accident: Part 1

***-ing* and *-ed* clauses**

1 Work as a class. The people in the pictures below were involved in an accident. Describe each of the people in one phrase, using the words below the picture and an *-ing* or an *-ed* clause. Example: Picture 1: *A young mother pushing a pram with a baby in it . . .*

1 A young mother . . . 4 An elderly man . . .

2 A teenager . . . 5 A boy and a girl . . .

3 A chauffeur . . . 6 A lorry . . .

2 Work in pairs or small groups. Choose a street in the place where you are learning English and imagine that the accident happened there. Say what each of the people in the accident were doing from any time before the accident until the accident happened. For example, where were they all going when the accident happened? Use the *-ing* and *-ed* clauses from 1 to say who the people are and use as many other *-ing* and *-ed* clauses as you naturally can.

Example: *The lorry loaded with bricks started its journey in south London . . . The teenager crossing the road was hurrying to school.*

2 The accident: Part 2

***-ing*, *-ed* and relative clauses**

1 Work as a class. Make sure you understand the vocabulary below. It will help you to describe the accident. Can you think of any other words you might need to describe an accident?

Vocabulary: slippery road, traffic lights, pedestrian crossing, ambulance crew, to swerve, to skid, to go too fast, to drive recklessly, to come round the corner, not looking where s/he is going

2 Work in pairs or groups. Describe the accident. You can use a drawing or diagram to help you, if you want to. Remember, all the people in the pictures in *The accident: Part 1* were involved. Use as many *-ing*, *-ed* and relative clauses as you naturally can. Use the past tense.
Examples:
The lorry loaded with bricks was out of control.
The motorbike, which had skidded on the wet slippery road, . . .

3 One pair or group describes the accident to the class. Note down any interesting uses of *-ing*, *-ed* and relative clauses.

3 The D I Y crossword

Relative clauses

1 Work in pairs or groups. Write crossword clues. Each clue must contain a relative pronoun introducing a relative clause. You must know the answers to your own clues.
Example:
Clue: A black and white bird which can swim but can't fly. Seven letters. Answer: Penguin.

2 Work in the same pairs or groups. Design a crossword from your crossword clues.

3 Work in the same pairs or groups. Give your crossword to another pair or group to do. Complete another pair or group's crossword.

D Accuracy practice

1 You are talking about a party you went to last week. Join the sentences using *whose.*

1 There was a tall man at the party. His wife could not come because she was ill.
2 There was a journalist there. Her work took her to lots of different countries.
3 I met a lot of new people at the party. I can't remember their names.
4 I talked to a woman. Her car had broken down on the way to the party.
5 I was introduced to a man. I had seen his brother on television the evening before.

2 Put in either *which* or *whose.* Christine is talking to a friend about her new job.

1 I'm working for a firm ____ main office is in London.
2 The firm, ____ employs five hundred people, makes video recorders.
3 My boss, ____ work takes him to a lot of other countries, has decided he needs an assistant in London. That's me.
4 I work mainly in the Finance Department, ____ is the smallest department in the firm.
5 The work, ____ increases a lot when the boss is away, is always interesting.

3 Put in a relative pronoun (*who, which, where, whose* or *that*).

1 The house ____ I lived as a child has been pulled down now.
2 Stop him! He's the man ____ stole my wallet.
3 There are many people ____ lives have been spoiled by that factory.
4 Is that the button ____ you pressed?
5 Could everybody ____ luggage has got lost please stay here?
6 The man ____ I saw last week said something totally different.
7 They have invented a television set ____ is as small as a watch.
8 My grandmother, ____ was an extraordinary woman, lived to the age of a hundred and fifteen.

4 Put the information in brackets into the sentence without using a relative pronoun. (Use an *-ing* or *-ed* clause.)

Example: A lorry has been stolen. (it was loaded with bricks)
A lorry loaded with bricks has been stolen.

1 A briefcase has been found in Room 253. (it belongs to the Managing Director)
2 That burglar is a neighbour of ours. (he was sentenced to five years in prison)
3 I heard some people in the street. (they were shouting)
4 The man was taken to hospital. (he was hurt in the accident)
5 The fence has been mended. (it was broken by the children)

15

Comparative and superlative adjectives and adverbs

A Starting activities

1 A look at the system

Comparative and superlative adjectives and adverbs

1 Work as a class. Put these comparative and superlative adjectives into two groups. In what way are the two groups different? Add one or two examples of your own to each group.

a cheaper, the cheapest
b more reliable, the most reliable
c newer, the newest
d more valuable, the most valuable
e more tired, the most tired
f easier, the easiest

2 Which words are missing?

a This dictionary is bigger ____ yours.
b This suitcase is just as big ____ the one I have at home.
c Having no money is ____ biggest problem he has at the moment.

3 What are the comparative and superlative forms of these words?

a often
b early
c smoothly
d long
e hard

When you have finished, look at Activity note 35 on page 146.

2 Comparative adverb building

Comparison of adverbs

1 Work as a class. List pairs of fictional or real people to talk about (for example, Indiana Jones and James Bond). In a separate column list verbs that you could use to compare them. In a third column list adverbs (not comparative adverbs). Example:

Indiana Jones and James Bond	*drive*	*dangerously*
	live	*fast*

2 Work in pairs. Make sentences using the verbs and adverbs from your list (or any others that you like) comparing the two people. Change the adverbs to comparative adverbs. Example: *Indiana Jones lives more dangerously than James Bond.*

3 Mine is just as good

Comparison of adjectives and adverbs

Work in pairs, A and B. Take turns to be A and B.

Person A: Choose one thing that you own. Try to sell it to B.

Person B: You do not want to buy whatever A is selling because you already have one which is just as good as or better than A's. For example, if it is a CD player yours is just as modern, if it is a watch yours keeps better time, if it is a car yours goes faster. Use as many comparatives as you can.

B Grammar guide

1 Comparative and superlative adjectives

- For one-syllable adjectives (like *rich*) the comparative is *-er than* and the superlative is *the -est.*
  *Buying the video is cheap**er than** paying for seats to see the film at the cinema.*
  *This was **the** cheap**est** box of chocolates in the shop.*
  One-syllable adjectives with one vowel followed by one consonant (like *big* or *sad*) double the consonant in the comparative and the superlative.
  big → bigger → the biggest   sad → sadder → the saddest
- Two- and three-syllable adjectives and adjectives ending in *-ed* have their comparative made with *more* and their superlative with *most.*
  I was more tired after the holiday than I was before it. (*-ed* adjective, comparative)
  She's the most intelligent person I know. (three-syllable adjective, superlative)
- These one-syllable adjectives have irregular comparatives and superlatives:
  good → better than → the best   bad → worse than → the worst
  far → further than (or *farther than*) *→ the furthest* (or *the farthest*).
- These two-syllable adjectives ending in *y* have the comparative *-ier than* and the superlative *the -iest*: *angry* (*angrier, angriest*), *busy, dirty, early, easy, friendly, funny, happy, lucky, pretty, silly, ugly.*
- These two-syllable adjectives have the comparative *-er than* and the superlative *the -est*: *narrow* (*narrower, narrowest*), *clever, simple, quiet.*
- Sometimes it is clear, or understood, what you are comparing something with, and then you do not need to use *than.*
  *This flat is bigger than that one, and it has **nicer** furniture.*

- Use *as . . . as* to compare things that are equal.
  My English is as good as his.
  To emphasize the equality, use *just as . . . as.*
  My suitcase is just as big as Derek's, so why are we using his?
- To say that there is not much difference between things use *a bit* or *a little.*
  Your car was a bit cheaper than mine.
  Make the difference even smaller with *only a bit* or *only a little.*
- To say there is a big difference use *far* or *much* or *a lot.*
  Your car was far/much cheaper than mine, and it's a lot faster.
  To make the difference even bigger use *very much* but NOT ~~*very far*~~.
- Use *the more . . . the -er* or *the more . . . the more* for two things happening together.
  The more you eat, the fuller you get.   The more I try, the less successful I am.
- And for the idea of something that goes on and on use two comparatives.
  He's getting fatter and fatter.   She's getting more and more dissatisfied.

2 Comparative and superlative adverbs

For the comparative and superlative of adverbs use *more* and *most.*
*She comes here **more often than** I do.*
*The engine runs **most smoothly** at speeds over sixty kilometres an hour.*
A few adverbs have the comparative *-er* and the superlative *-est*: *early* (*earlier, earliest*), *fast, hard, late, long, near* and *soon.* Other irregular adverbs are:
badly → worse → worst; little → less → least; much → more → most.

C Activities

1 A better job

Comparative and superlative adjectives and adverbs

1 Work in pairs or small groups. Write down five jobs (for example, accountant, bricklayer) you would like to do and five jobs you would not like to do.

2 Work in the same pairs or small groups. A friend of yours wants to change from one of the jobs on your list to one of the others. Say how your friend's life would be changed by comparing the jobs in terms of: salary, conditions, time to spend with the family, job satisfaction, job security, value to society. Keep comparing jobs until you have compared five pairs of jobs. Use as many comparative and superlative adjectives and adverbs as you naturally can. Examples: *The salary will be higher. You will be away from home more often.*

3 Work as a class. Tell the other people in the class about the jobs you compared. List sentences comparing the jobs that people in the class used.

2 Dinner with the famous

Comparative and superlative adjectives and adverbs

1 Work on your own. You have decided to invite a lot of famous people to a party. Write down the names of the five famous people you would most like to invite.

2 Work in pairs or small groups. Persuade your partner or the other people in the group to invite the people on your list, not the people on his/her/their lists, by comparing the people on the two lists. Use as many comparative and superlative adjectives and adverbs as you naturally can. Use *far* or *much* for emphasis. Example: *Woody Allen is far more interesting than Queen Elizabeth.*

3 Work as a class. List sentences comparing the people that the class used and try to think of more ways of comparing the people. Decide, as a class, which five people in the world you would most like to invite for dinner.

3 World records

Superlative adjectives

1 Work in pairs or small groups. Guess what the world records below are for. You can make your guesses as wild and improbable as you like. Example: (a) *The biggest carrot ever grown.*

World records

a 8 feet $3\frac{3}{4}$ inches (263.5 cm)
b 200 lb (91 kg) in 9 days
c 69
d 4
e None for 182 days.
f Papua New Guinea.
g *I Believe* by Frankie Lane
h 1.2 inches
i 104 per 100,000 of the population, or 370 per day
j 1.6 billion

2 Work as a class. Compare your wild guesses with those of other people in the class. List the funniest or wildest or most interesting wild guesses. (The real answers are in Activity note 66 on page 158.)

D Accuracy practice

1 Put in the comparative of the adjectives and adverbs in brackets, and *than*, where necessary.

1 This oven heats up ____ the one I'm used to. (slowly)
2 Flying is ____ going by train. (cheap)
3 It's strange that this blue dress is ____ that one because it is made of far ____ material. (expensive, bad)
4 At the moment, getting over your illness is ____ finishing your work. (important)
5 There's no time limit, so try not to write ____ you have to. (fast)
6 Sometimes I think he comes ____ everyone else does just to annoy me. (late)
7 He comes here a lot ____ he used to. (often)
8 Shane is quite a lot ____ he was when he was young. (friendly)

2 Finish the sentences using *as . . . as*, *the more . . . the -er*, or *the more . . . the more/less*.

1 John and Mary are equally good guitarists.
John plays the guitar ____________
2 If your salary goes up, the amount you pay in tax also goes up.
The more your salary goes up, ____________
3 You cannot say that one of them is cleverer than the other. They get the same exam results.
They are ____________ each other.
4 If you do a lot of work now, you will feel happier about the examination.
The more work you do now, ____________
5 If a lot of people help now, we will have less to do later.
The more people help now, ____________

3 Complete the questions using the superlative of the adjectives and adverbs in brackets.

1 Of the people in the class, who is ____ (interesting)?
2 In which continent is ____ (long) river in the world?
3 Who is ____ (fast) runner in the world, at the moment?
4 Which opera singer sings ____ (beautiful), do you think?
5 In which museum, in which city, is ____ (big) diamond in the world?

4 Put in the most appropriate comparative or superlative adjective or adverb.

1 She's only been doing the job for a month. Of all the staff she has ____ experience.
2 That was a terrible meal. I think it was one of ____ meals I've ever eaten.
3 We have been walking for an hour already. It's ____ I thought to the next village.
4 I have to start work ____ you do. You don't start until eight but sometimes I start before seven in the morning.
5 He's so noisy. It's a lot ____ when he isn't here.

Phrasal verbs I: by verb (*come, get, go* etc.)

A Starting activities

1 How many combinations do you know?

Building phrasal verbs

1 Work in pairs or groups. Each pair or group chooses one of the grids below. Copy out the grid you have chosen. Put a cross on the grid if a combination is impossible and put a tick for each combination which is possible. For example, on grid 1, ~~*do off*~~ is impossible but *get off* is possible. Put each possible combination into a sentence, like this: *I usually get off the bus at that bus stop over there.*

Grid 1	get	go	make	do
off	✓			×
back				
up				

Grid 2	come	take	go	make
up				
in				
to				

Grid 3	take	put	do	get
to				
back				
up				

When you have finished, look at Activity note 27 on page 143.

2 Work as a class. Read out your sentences. List sentences under each verb used (for example, *get, go*). Underline the phrasal verb in each sentence.

2 Private conversations

Phrasal verbs in spoken English

1 Work in pairs. Working together write one of the dialogues below. Use the list of phrasal verbs below to give you ideas and use at least three of the phrasal verbs from the list in your dialogue.

Dialogue 1: A boyfriend and girlfriend are having an argument. She is angry with him for something he has done. Example: *We aren't getting on very well together, are we?*

Dialogue 2: A secretary and a boss are talking. The secretary says the boss is giving her/him too much work and the boss says the secretary is too slow. Example: *I'm sorry, but I need to put some of these letters off until later.*

Dialogue 3: Two workers at a factory or office are planning the firm's annual day out. Example: *Have you come up with any ideas for the trip?*

List of phrasal verbs

take on (+ something)
go out with (+ someone)
get through (work)
get on
take back
put off
put away
come back
make up
get on with (+ something)
take down (a letter)
get up to (+ something bad)
take to
come round
get round to
get together
make up for
come up with

2 Work in pairs. Read your dialogue aloud to another pair. Listen to the other pair's dialogue and write down the sentences with the three phrasal verbs in them.

B Grammar guide

1 What are phrasal verbs?

Phrasal verbs are verbs like *put* followed by adverb particles like *on* (for example, *put on* in the sentence *Put your coat on*). Some people also call verb + preposition combinations phrasal verbs. The verb can be followed by a particle and a preposition, for example, *I won't put* ***up with*** *this.* The same phrasal verb can have different meanings, for example, *take off* in *Take your coat off* and *The plane took off late.*

2 Phrasal verbs with a direct object (transitive)

- Inseparable (the direct object always follows the particle)

come across *I wasn't looking for it. I came across it by chance.*
get away with *The criminals were never caught. They got away with the murder.*
get on with (+ someone) *We fight all the time. We just don't get on with each other.*
get on with (+ something) *Can you get on with the housework while I go down to the supermarket, please?*
get over *Susan has got over her cold and she's feeling fine now.*
get round to *I did everything else you asked me to do. I just didn't get round to cleaning the windows.*
get up to *I don't know what Henry is getting up to in the kitchen, but I can smell something burning.*
go in for *He's gone in for the exam again and I think he'll pass this time.*
make up for *I hope this present makes up for missing the party.*
put up with *I'm not putting up with bad service like that.*
take to *She's nice. I took to her as soon as I saw her.*

- Separable

Sometimes the direct object can come between the verb and the adverb particle. If the direct object is a pronoun (like *it* or *them*) it must come between the verb and the particle. For example, *Can you do my dress up?* OR *Can you do up my dress?* But *Can you do it up?* (NOT ~~*do up it*~~)

do up *Can you do my dress up? I can't reach the zip at the back.*
make up *That is not true. He made the whole story up.*
put off *I've got a lot to do at the moment. Can we put the meeting off until later, please?*
put up *We've got a spare bed. I can put Jenny up for the night.*
take away *Jim, ask the waiter to take all these glasses away. There's no more room on the table.*
take over *Jacksons own Smith PLC. They took the firm over in June.*
take up *When did you take the violin up? You play very well.*

3 Phrasal verbs with no direct object (intransitive)

come round *Sally told Guy to come round whenever he wants. So now he's at Sally's flat every evening.*
come up *We discussed Taylor and Loach for the job but your name didn't come up. Nobody thought of you, I'm afraid.*
get by *Can you move, please? I can't get by.*
go ahead *Even if it's bad news, go ahead and tell me.*
go off *Smell this milk. I think it's gone off.*
make up *I don't want to fight. Let's kiss and make up.*
take off *The plane took off smoothly.*

C Activities

1 Phrasal verb bingo

Discovering more phrasal verbs

1 Work on your own. Make a bingo card like this:

a Take a piece of paper and write three verbs on the left in large letters.

b Write three particles on the right of the piece of paper in large letters. It must be possible to combine all of the verbs with all of the particles.

c Ask the person next to you to check that your three verbs and your three particles can combine. In some uses the particles may be prepositions but do not worry about this. The most useful verbs and particles for you to learn are listed below.

Verbs

be	*break*	*bring*	*come*	*do*
fall	*find*	*get*	*give*	*go*
help	*let*	*look*	*make*	*put*
send	*stand*	*take*	*tear*	*throw*
turn				

Particles

about	*across*	*along*	*around*	*away*
back	*by*	*forward*	*down*	*in*
off	*on*	*out*	*over*	*through*
to	*under*	*up*	*with*	

2 Tear the paper in half. Give your verbs to your teacher and keep the three particles. Your teacher will now call out verbs from the pieces of paper he or she has been given by the class. If one of your three particles can combine with a verb that the teacher calls out, shout 'Bingo'. The first person to shout 'Bingo' gets a chance to make a sentence with that verb + particle combination. The first person to make three correct sentences with her or his three particles wins.

2 A day in the life

Learning and using phrasal verbs

1 Work in pairs or groups. Write a day in the life of one of the following: a film star, a homeless person, a cat. Use as many different phrasal verbs as you can in natural English. You can use the list of phrasal verbs below to help you and to give you ideas but you do not have to use all of them.

Example: *I get up at dawn and eat whatever I come across first for breakfast.*

List of phrasal verbs

get up	*come across*	*come up with*
get round to	*look forward to*	*put away*
turn on/off	*throw away*	*throw out*
turn up	*get across*	*get on with*
make for	*make out*	*make up for*
put up with	*take away*	

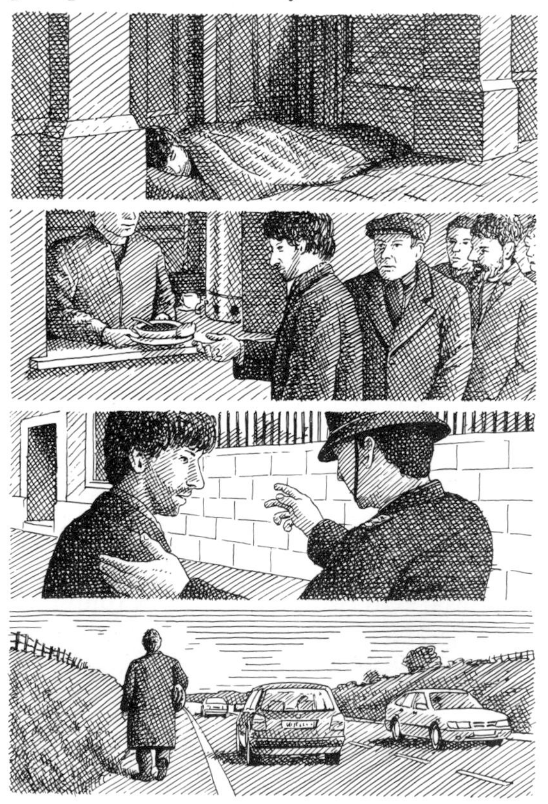

2 Work as a class. Read your day in the life to the class. Listen to other people reading theirs and list sentences with phrasal verbs in them.

D Accuracy practice

1 **Put in the correct form of these phrasal verbs:** ***go in for, put off, get up to, take over, come round, make up for, get away with, put up.***

1. He ____ ____ to my house after work yesterday and stayed for two hours.
2. We can't ____ this ____ any longer. We must do it now.
3. Camilla's ____ ____ ____ the exam next week.
4. I must write to Anna when I get back. It was nice of her to ____ me ____ for the night.
5. She's not going to ____ ____ ____ telling all those lies about Wayne.
6. I've got a better job since Mersons ____ my company ____, which ____ ____ ____ having more work to do.
7. What's the baby ____ ____ ____ with that bottle? Put it down, Kylie!

2 **Complete these sentences with** ***get*** **and these words:** ***on with*** **(×2),** ***by, round to, over.***

1. I've been so busy, I just didn't ____ ____ ____ writing any letters.
2. She fights with her little brother the whole time. They just don't ____ ____ ____ each other.
3. Can you ____ ____ ____ the exercise I asked you to do, please? I'll be back in a minute.
4. Can you let me through, please? I can't ____ ____.
5. He was upset when his girlfriend walked out but he'll ____ ____ it.

3 **Complete these sentences with a phrasal verb. Use these verbs:** ***put, take, make, go, do.***

1. We've been sitting here with our seatbelts on for ten minutes. When is this plane going to ____ ____?
2. The story sounded good but I'm sure he ____ it ____. It just can't be true.
3. The boss says it's OK. We can ____ ____ with the plan.
4. What's that smell? Some food must have ____ ____.
5. I'm not going to ____ ____ ____ that noise any longer. I can't get to sleep at night.
6. She only ____ ____ tennis six months ago and she's really good at it.
7. They had another big argument last week but they ____ it ____ the next day.
8. I can't ____ this belt ____. It's too small for me.

4 **Write sentences using the phrasal verbs in brackets.**

1. We can't/them/because we haven't got room. (put up)
2. Did you/Ronald/when you were in Washington? (come across)
3. What's wrong with these buttons? Can you/them/please? (do up)
4. Can you/these buttons/please? (do up)
5. The dustmen/the rubbish/before seven this morning. (take away)

17

Advice (*should, had better*) and necessity (*need, don't have to*)

A Starting activities

1 Dangerous situations

had better, had better not

Work in pairs. Here are some dangerous situations. Imagine that they are happening or have happened in the place where you are learning English: fire, flood, the roof falling in, a dangerous criminal holding a hostage in the basement (he has escaped from prison), a wild animal running loose in the car park (it has escaped from a zoo). Add to the list if you wish. Say what it would be best to do in all the situations. Make as many sentences as you can with *we had better* and *we had better not.*
Examples:
We had better get some buckets for all this water.
We had better not try to catch the lion without help.

2 We need to think of a name for the company

Necessity with *need to*

Work in pairs or as a class. You are starting a new company. Decide what the company is going to do or make. List sentences about everything you need to do before the company can start trading. Use *need to.* Use the vocabulary below to help you.
Example: *We need to think of a name for the company.*

Vocabulary: staff, premises, logo, bank loan, machinery

3 They should have come earlier

should have, need not have

Work as a class. For each of the pictures, say a sentence using *should have* + past participle or *need not have* + past participle. Example (for picture 1): *We need not have brought towels. The hotel has provided them.*

B Grammar guide

1 Advice

- We use *should* to say what we think is best for another person. We usually use it when we are talking about our own feelings about the situation.
  It's a good book. You should read it. (Because I think you would like the book.)
  You're looking tired. You shouldn't work so hard. (Because I think that is what is best for you.)
- You can ask for advice using *should.*
  Should we tell her?
  Do you think we should wait any longer?
- We use *should* with *have* + past participle to say that in the past somebody did not do something that was the best thing for them.
  We've eaten all the food now. You should have come home earlier. (= You didn't come home earlier but you should have.)
  The negative is *should not have* + past participle.
  We've eaten all the food now. You shouldn't have come home so late. (= You came home late but you should not have.)
- *Had better* is another way of giving advice. We use it to say 'It would be better if you . . .'. The past form *had* is always used, although the meaning is present or future, not past. We use an infinitive after *had better.*
  You'd better tell Jim you've borrowed his cassettes, or he'll be angry with you.
  You had better not bring your bicycle indoors.

2 Necessity

- Use *need to* to say that it is necessary to do something.
  We need to get a visa before we go to the USA.
- To say that something is not necessary, use *don't need to, don't have to* or *needn't. Needn't* is not followed by *to.*
  You needn't apologize. (OR *You don't need to apologize.* OR *You don't have to apologize.*)
- When something was not necessary in the past use *did not need to, did not have to* or *need not have.* When a speaker uses *did not need to* or *did not have to* we do not know if the action happened or not, only that it was not necessary.
  They did not need to pay. (We do not know if they paid or not.)
  They did not have to wait for the bus. (We do not know if they waited or not.)
  But when *need not have* + past participle is used, we know that something happened and it was not necessary.
  They need not have waited for the bus. (We know that they waited and that it was not necessary.)
  They need not have brought towels. The hotel provided them. (We know that they brought towels and that it was not necessary.)

C Activities

1 Dear Doris . . .

Giving advice with *should, should not, had better* and *had better not*

1 Work on your own. Doris is an 'Agony Aunt' who works for a magazine. People write to her with their personal problems and she replies, giving advice. Think of a problem. Write a one-paragraph letter to Doris telling her about the problem as if you were the person with the problem. (Four or five sentences will be enough.)

2 Work as a class. Read your letter to Doris out to the class. Discuss other people's letters and give advice, using *should, should not, had better* and *had better not.*

2 Wrong turnings

***should have* and *shouldn't have* + past participle**

1 Work in pairs. The story of Graham and Davina Alison is in the Activity notes section. Some people would say that Graham and Davina took some wrong turnings in life and made some mistakes. But they were right some of the time. First read Activity note 57 on page 155, then decide together what you think they should have done and should not have done.

2 Work as a class. Did other pairs think the same as you and your partner did about Graham and Davina? List all the times when most of the class thought that either Graham or Davina should have done something different.

3 We did it together

needed to, did not need to, did not have to, need not have

1 Work in pairs or small groups. You did or made something together. See the pictures below for ideas. Now you are both going to give a talk about how you did it. Plan the talk together using *needed to, did not need to, did not have to, need not have* as often as you realistically can. Examples:
We needed to learn to edit film.
We didn't have to buy the film ourselves.

Making a motorbike from a kit

Writing a biography

Making a video

Writing a cookery book

2 Work in the same pairs or small groups. Give your talk to the class.

D Accuracy practice

1 Complete the sentences. Use *should/had better* or *shouldn't/had better not.*

1 You ____ give up smoking, you know. It's bad for you.
2 Tell Jane she ____ work so hard. She is overdoing it.
3 You ____ get some sleep. You look tired out.
4 You ____ say that to Sharon. She'll be angry with you.
5 You ____ try to lift that by yourself. It's heavy.

2 Ask for advice using *Should I..* You want advice about:

1 which restaurant to go to, the Indian one or the Chinese one.
2 whether to take the motorbike or go by bus.
3 whether to cook dinner or buy a take-away meal.
4 whether to finish your homework or go out.
5 which shirt to wear, the striped one or the pink one.

3 Write sentences saying what *he/she should* or *shouldn't have done.*

1 He left the chicken in the oven for three hours. It only needed two hours to cook.
2 The saw she used to cut the wood was not sharp enough.
3 Alan had just a small cut on his knee but he called an ambulance.
4 Hettie did not tell her until it was too late.
5 Gavin only started working for his exams a week before he took them.

4 Complete the sentences. Use *need to, doesn't/don't need to, doesn't/don't have to* or *needn't.* Write all possible answers.

1 Jim, you ____ buy a newspaper. Sarah's got one we can read.
2 You ____ fill in one of those pink forms over there.
3 There is a meeting for people who failed the examination. Jim passed so he ____ come.
4 There ____ be a live band at the party. We can play our own records.
5 We ____ buy any sugar. We've got enough.

5 Write sentences saying what these people *needn't have done.*

Example: James did some shopping but Sue had bought a meal already.
James needn't have gone shopping.

1 Arthur was worried because Gemma was late coming home. But she got home safely.
2 Beverley handed her homework in although it wasn't due until the following week.
3 Eric brought his guitar to the party but there were plenty of CDs.
4 Lily phoned the police because she thought someone had stolen her chequebook. Later she found the chequebook in a drawer.

18

Future time: *going to*, *will*, present progressive and present simple

A Starting activities

1 She's seeing her doctor next week

Present progressive

1 Work in pairs. Think of three well-known people or three people in the room. Use present progressive sentences to tell your partner about their appointments for these times: this evening, tomorrow morning, next week, next month. Use the verbs and the ideas for appointments below to help you. Example: *Maria is seeing her doctor next week.*

Verbs: *go, meet, see, have a talk/meeting with*

Ideas for appointments: doctor, dentist, optician, bank manager, dress designer, tax adviser, accountant, architect, business manager, boss, the President, President of the fan club

2 Work as a class. Listen to other people's suggestions for appointments. Are there any that you think are wrong? Example: *No, Maria isn't seeing her doctor next week. She's having her hair done.*

2 Trapped

***going to* and the present progressive**

1 Work in pairs. Helen and her boyfriend John were travelling round the world together. Unfortunately, they could not get out of a certain country for six months. (Why not?) During this time they made some important decisions. When they finally got out they told their friends about their plans for the future.

Imagine that you are friends of Helen and John and make sentences about their intentions using *going to* or *not going to.* Use the ideas below to help you. Example: *They're going to get married.*
Ideas: have a big party, get married, buy a flat in town, leave/change jobs, have a holiday, travel abroad again

2 Work in the same pairs. It is three months later. This time one of you is Helen or John and the other one is a friend. The friend asks questions about Helen and John's intentions using *going to.* Helen or John answers with information about the couple's firm plans using the present progressive, like this:

FRIEND	*Are you going to get married?*
HELEN/JOHN	*Yes, we're getting married on 15 July in London.*

3 A fortune teller

will* and *going to

1 Work in pairs. One of you is a fortune teller first, then the other one has a turn. The fortune teller looks at his or her partner's hand and makes predictions about the future. Use *will/won't* or *going to/not going to.* Invent your partner's future but say only nice things! Say things about your partner's future career, love-life, luck and money situation and at least one surprise. Examples: *You will marry an Italian. You're going to get a new car soon.*

2 Work as a class. Tell the class some of your predictions and write down a few of the nicest predictions that other people made.

B Grammar guide

1 Present progressive

Use the present progressive to describe firm plans for the future.
The President is visiting London next week. (This is arranged.)
I'm seeing the doctor next week. (I have an appointment.)
We're moving to a flat in London. (We have made all the arrangements.)

2 *going to*

- Use *going to* to describe future intentions. Intentions are not as definite as firm plans. You have decided what you want to do in the future, but you have not made firm plans, appointments or arrangements.
  The President is going to spend more time with his family. (No arrangements have been made and no definite times have been decided.)
  I still have a pain. I'm going to see a doctor. (I have not made an appointment yet.)
  We're definitely going to buy a little flat in London. (We are looking at possible flats. We want to buy one.)
  NOTE You can sometimes use the present progressive or *going to* with no difference in meaning.
  Isn't it marvellous, we're getting married!
  Isn't it marvellous, we're going to get married!
- A prediction is what you think will happen in the future. Use *going to* for predictions when you can see now that something is going to happen. (In other words you have 'present evidence' that something is going to happen.)
  Look out! It's going to fall. *Look at those clouds. It's going to rain.*

3 *will*

- Use *will/won't* for predictions when you have no present evidence.
  In a hundred years' time we will all travel everywhere by helicopter.
  The train service won't be any better than it is now.
  You can often use either *will* or *going to* for predictions with very little difference in meaning.
  Fortune teller: (I can see in your hand that) *You are going to get married next year.*
  Fortune teller: (I know because I can see the future that) *You will get married next year.*
- Use *will* when something in the future is inevitable, in other words it is outside anybody's control.
  Next year I will be twenty-eight. *It will be spring soon.*
- Use *will* when you make a decision about something at the moment of speaking. It is not a plan of any sort, it is an idea you have just thought of. The contracted form *'ll* is usually used.
  OK, if we can't have a picnic, we'll stay in and watch a video.
  I'll do the washing up, if you like.
- Use *shall/shan't* and not *will/won't* for suggestions or to ask for advice. *Shall* is usually used with *I* or *we*, not with *you, he, she* or *it*.
  Shall we go out this evening?

4 Present simple

Use the present simple when you see something as a fact. In future time, 'facts' are usually regular events, timetables and the times that buildings open and close.
The train leaves at ten o'clock.

C Activities

1 A poem kit

will **for predicting**

Work in pairs or groups. Write four sentences that start with *When I'm old I'll . . .* Cut or tear the paper so that there is only one sentence on each piece of paper. Pass the pieces of paper around until each pair or group has four sentences that they did not write. Rewrite the sentences as a four-sentence poem. Only the first line has *When I'm old . . .* The other three lines start with *I'll.* The poem does not have to rhyme but read the lines aloud for a good rhythm. Here is an example:
When I'm old I'll have cornflakes for tea (no teeth you know).
I'll walk carefully,
I'll be happy, you'll see.
I'll play music for you and me.

2 Our town

will **for predicting; present simple for facts in the future**

1 Work in pairs or groups. Quickly draw the main streets in the centre of the town where you are having this lesson. Draw in any important places you can think of, like the Town Hall or a park. Then draw it all again as you think it will be in a hundred years' time. Discuss what the town will look like in a hundred years' time and what changes there will be, using the *will* future only. Examples: *The Town Hall will be a computer centre. There will be a helicopter landing pad in the park.*

2 Work in pairs or groups. Using the drawing of the town in one hundred years' time, take it in turns to be a tour guide. Imagine that you are taking your partner or the rest of your group round your town in a hundred years' time. Tell them about everything they can see. Use some present simple sentences for future time where you can, like this: *This is the helicopter landing pad. The next helicopter leaves from here in five minutes.*

3 Improving your classroom

going to **(for intentions) and *will* (for ideas you have just thought of)**

1 Work as a class. Half the class is Team A and the other half of the class is Team B. Team A and Team B have five minutes to think of possible improvements to the classroom. You can talk to anybody in your own team and write down ideas. Examples: *Paint the walls blue. Have armchairs in here.*

2 Someone from Team A says an intended improvement using *going to.* Example: *We're going to paint the walls blue.*
Team A gets one point if the *going to* sentence is correct.

Someone from Team B makes an objection or points out a problem. Example: *You can't paint the walls blue, there's no blue paint.*
Team B gets one point if the sentence is correct.

Someone from Team A must think of something spontaneously and say a correct sentence with *will.* Example: *OK, we'll paint the walls green then.*
Team A gets one point if the *will* sentence is correct.

Then Team B has a turn to start by saying one of their intended improvements.

4 She's leaving home

Present progressive, *will, going to*

There is a song by *The Beatles* called *She's Leaving Home.* It is about a daughter who leaves her family home for the first time to go and live somewhere else. This activity is about the same situation. Work in pairs, A and B.
Person A: Read Activity note 13 on page 139.
Person B: Read Activity note 51 on page 153.

D Accuracy practice

1 Write complete sentences. Use the present progressive or *going to*. Use both where both are possible.

1. I/buy/a car as soon as I have enough money.
2. Can you meet Richard at the station, please? He/arrive/at nine o'clock on the train from Oxford.
3. Her boyfriend/not/come/until next week.
4. You/definitely/pass/the exam.
5. /you/work/at home next week?

2 Complete the sentences. Use *will*, *won't*, or *shall*.

1. What ____ we do this evening?
2. I don't know what he ____ do. He won't tell me anything.
3. I'm tired. I think I ____ go to bed.
4. She ____ get there in time. She set off too late.
5. It's a formal party, so what ____ we wear?

3 Write complete sentences. Use *will*, *won't* or *going to*.

1. That parcel looks heavy. I/take/it to the Post Office for you.
2. I know what! I/not/take/the car at all. I/walk/.
3. It's Jane's birthday in August. She/be/sixteen.
4. He/meet/Mary at the station. He told her yesterday that he would.
5. Look at those clouds. It/rain/.

4 Complete the sentences. Use *will*, *going to*, the present progressive or the present simple. Sometimes there is more than one possible answer.

1. We've agreed that Jim ____ (buy) the food for the party, and I ____ (cook) it.
2. Quick! The museum ____ (close) at half-past five. It says so in the guidebook.
3. I know! I ____ (drive) Tina to the station now.
4. We ____ (not/know) the answer to that until next week.
5. I've made an appointment at the dentist's. I ____ (see) her on Tuesday.
6. This train ____ (stop) at every station between here and London.
7. Louise can't come with us. She ____ (take) the car to the garage at four o'clock.

5 Two teenagers, Angela and Darren, were going out together. But then Angela found another boyfriend, Richard. Complete Darren's letter to Angela. Use *will*, *going to* or the present progressive. Sometimes more than one answer is possible.

I [1] ____ (not/phone) you any more, because you asked me not to, but I am writing you a quick note as I've got nothing else to do at the moment. [2] ____ (you/go) to the school dance with Richard? I [3] ____ (not/go). Or at least maybe I [4] ____ (go) but I probably [5] ____ (not/dance) with anybody. I've decided that I [6] ____ (not/play) any more *Deep Pit* records because I think of you every time I hear one. I [7] ____ (stop) now. The lesson [8] ____ (start) soon. I am sure that you and Richard [9] ____ (be) really happy together. I [10] ____ (phone) you next week, if that's OK.

19

Possibility, probability and deduction: *may, might, could; should, ought to; must, can't*

A Starting activities

1 I must be dreaming!

must **and** ***can't*** **for deduction in the present**

Work in pairs or groups. Say as many *must* and *can't* sentences as you can think of for each of the pictures below. Give reasons for your deductions. Example (picture 1): *He must be a car thief. He's breaking into that car. He can't be the owner of that car. He hasn't got a key.*

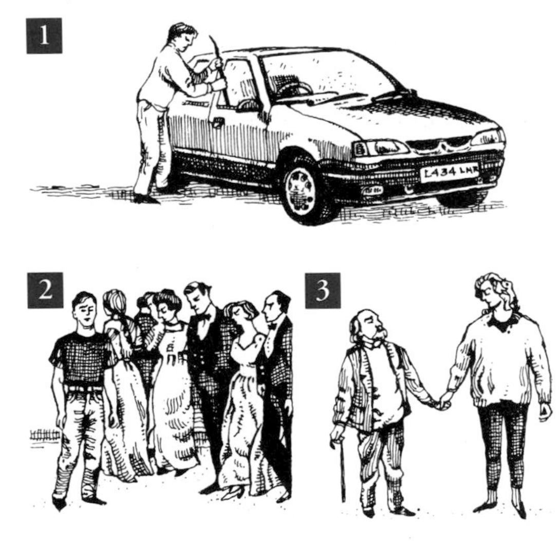

2 Which is which? I

Possibility, probability and deduction in the present and future

Work as a class. Complete the grid. Use *may, might* or *could* for possibility and *should* or *ought to* for probability. Use *must* or *can't* for deduction. Part of the grid is completed for you.

Present and future time

	Positive	Negative	Question
Possibility	*He may/ might/ could be in London*		
Probability			*Should he be in London by now?*
Deduction			

When you have finished, look at Activity note 52 on page 153.

3 Which is which? II

Possibility, probability and deduction in the past

Work as a class or in pairs. Complete this grid in the same way that you completed the grid above.

Past time

	Positive	Negative	Question
Possibility	*He may/ might/ could have gone to London*		
Probability			*Should he have been in London?*
Deduction			

When you have finished, look at Activity note 15 on page 140.

B Grammar guide

1 Possibility

- To talk about a present or future possibility we use *may*, *might* or *could* + infinitive without *to*.
  There's a parcel here. It could be from Bill. *It might snow next week.*
  NOTE *May*, *might* and *could* can be followed by *be* + the *-ing* form for present and future possibility.
  They could be watching television. *I may be going to Oxford tomorrow.*
- To talk about a possibility in the past we use *may*, *might* or *could* + *have* + the past participle.
  He could have got lost.
- Questions about possibility in the past, present and future are formed with *could* or *might* but not *may*.
  Might she have been the wrong person to ask? (past)
  Could the answer be 'six'? (present)
  Might she be coming tomorrow? (future)
- For possibility with a negative in the past, present and future use *may not* or *might not*. The contraction *mightn't* is often used in speech. *Could not* is not used for negative possibility.
  He mightn't have wanted to buy any. (past)
  'Six' may not be the answer. (present)
  They might not come tomorrow. *They might not be coming tomorrow.* (future)

2 Probability

If something is possible, it might happen. If something is probable, it is likely to happen.

- To talk about a present or future probability, use *should* or *ought to*.
  She should be on her way home now. She always leaves work at six.
  This means, for example, that she has usually left her office by now and we expect her to arrive home soon.
  NOTE *should/ought to* can be followed by *be* + the *-ing* form.
  Their plane ought to be taking off about now.
- To talk about a probability in the past we use *should have* or *ought to have* + past participle. Use *should have* or *ought to have* + past participle to talk about:

a something that you expected to happen in the past. You do not know definitely if it happened or not, but you think it probably did.
They should have reached London by now.
In this example, according to the timetable they have arrived in London but you don't know definitely whether they are there or not.

b something that you thought would happen but that did not happen.
She should have passed her driving test easily. She's a good driver.
In this example, she did not pass her test.

3 Deduction

- We use *must* when we have a good reason for believing something.
  He's breaking that car window. He must be a car thief.
  We use *can't* when we have a good reason for not believing something.
  He's too young. He can't be in the army.
- For deduction in the past we use *must* or *can't/couldn't* + *have* + past participle.
  He must have been delayed. *He can't/couldn't have read my letter properly.*

C Activities

1 The sad story of Susie Jones

may, might, could for possibility in the past

1 Work in pairs or groups. Read the sad story of Susie Jones below and make as many sentences (positive and negative) as you can to explain the possible reasons:
why Susie's marriage didn't take place,
why she left the country,
why she had to leave her job in television,
why she devoted her life to abandoned animals.
Example: *She might have discovered that her fiancé was already married.*

The sad story of Susie Jones
Susie Jones was going to get married, but the day before the wedding she suddenly called it off. She left the country and lived abroad for several years. When she came back she got a very good job as a television producer but she resigned unexpectedly six months later. She devoted the rest of her lonely life to caring for abandoned animals.

2 Work as a class. Listen to other people's ideas and write down some of the possible reasons for Susie's actions.

3 Work in pairs or groups. Rewrite the story of Susie Jones putting in some of the sentences you wrote down.

2 The *Marie Celeste*

must and *can't/couldn't* for deduction in the past

1 Work on your own. Read the story of the *Marie Celeste.*

The *Marie Celeste* was a sailing ship. It was sailing from New York to Italy in 1872. There was a crew of eight on board as well as the captain's wife and daughter. A month after the journey started, another ship noticed the *Marie Celeste* floating off the coast of Spain. When the sailors from the other ship went on board, they found everything in place on the *Marie Celeste.* The sails were set, the table was laid for dinner, there was plenty of food in the kitchen. There were toys on the floor in the captain's cabin, as if his little daughter had just been playing. The crew's clothes were hanging up neatly and their boots were all in place. But there was nobody on board at all. And nobody has ever discovered what happened to the captain and his family or the crew.

2 Work in pairs or small groups. Discuss what could have happened to the people on board the *Marie Celeste.* Make as many positive and negative deductions as possible. Give reasons for your deductions, where necessary, like this: *There can't have been a storm because the sails were set. The captain must have tried to save his family.*

3 Work as a class. Listen to other people's ideas and list some sentences with *must* and *can't/couldn't* for deduction in the past.

3 Brilliant James

should, ought to for probability in the past

Work as a class. 'Brilliant James' came from a rich family. He could read when he was three and he was very good-looking. Despite all these advantages, he is now unemployed and homeless. In one column, list everything that you expected 'Brilliant James' to do in life but which he didn't do. Write *should have/ought to have* + past participle sentences. In another column, write what actually happened, like this:

Expected	**What happened**
He ought to have done well at school.	He failed all his exams.

D Accuracy practice

1 **Complete the sentences. Use *may, might* or *could* + *be* + the *-ing* form of the verb in brackets (e.g. *may be doing*). More than one answer is possible.**

1. 'Where's Calley?' 'I'm not sure, she ____ (watch) television.'
2. 'Are you coming on Saturday or Sunday?' 'I don't know. I ____ (not/come) this weekend at all.'
3. My parents want to come, so we ____ (take) them with us.
4. ____ (John/leave) his job and going to another company?
5. Harry ____ (not/play) in the team tomorrow. He hurt his leg last week.

2 **Complete the sentences. Use *may/might/could* + *have* + the past participle of the verb in brackets.**

1. 'Why didn't Kim come?' 'I don't know. She ____ (forget).'
2. 'Why didn't Roger answer the doorbell?' 'He ____ (not/hear) it.'
3. 'How did that stain get on the carpet?' 'I'm not sure. The baby ____ (drop) food on it.'
4. John thinks Mr Wright ____ (tell) police.
5. He ____ (go out) without telling me; but he usually tells me.

3 **Complete the sentences. Use *should/ought to* + *have* + the past participle of the verb in brackets.**

1. Ben's late. He ____ (be) here ages ago.
2. I hope she isn't waiting for a bus. I ____ (tell) her there are no buses today.
3. The other team weren't very good, so our team really ____ (win).
4. That parcel was posted last month. It ____ (arrive) a long time ago.
5. It's too late to revise for the exam now. You ____ (do) more work earlier on.

4 **Complete the sentences. Use *must* or *can't/couldn't* + *have* + the past participle of the verb in brackets (e.g. *must have done*).**

1. You ____ (be) at the disco last night, it was closed.
2. I told you that before. You ____ (be) listening.
3. The light's on. They ____ (get) home before we did.
4. You know where the park is, don't you? You ____ (pass) it on your way here.
5. She ____ (go) very far. She's left her bicycle here.

5 **These sentences about possibility, probability and deduction are wrong. Correct them.**

1. ~~I don't know who gave me this book. It should have been my parents.~~
2. ~~Mr Ridley says he had left the building before the money was stolen, but may he have come back later?~~
3. ~~She shouldn't be out so late. Look at her, she mustn't be more than fifteen.~~
4. ~~You must have been Arthur's sister. Hello, I'm Jim.~~
5. ~~I've just phoned Henry's parents. They say he's just left them. The journey takes two hours. It's five o'clock now, so he really may arrive here by seven.~~

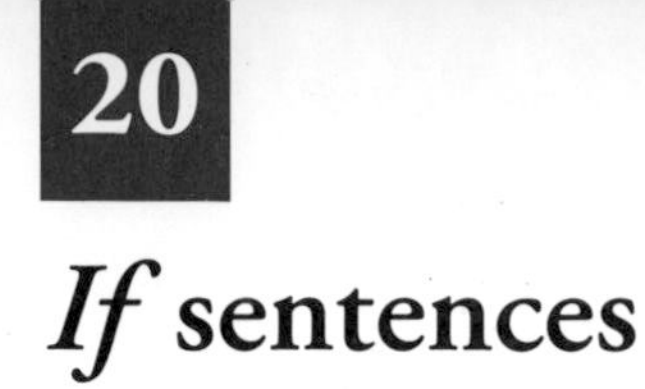

If sentences

A Starting activities

1 A perfect couple

If with something that is always true
(*if* + present simple, + present simple)

1 Work as a class. You know a perfect couple, Mr and Mrs . . . (give them a name). List the ways that they are perfect using the present simple tense, like this:

Mrs . . .	**Mr . . .**
She is good at making things.	*He is kind.*
She works hard.	*He smiles a lot.*
She buys him nice presents.	*He brings her breakfast in bed.*

2 Work in pairs. Use the sentences the class listed to give you ideas for *if* sentences that are always true. Write down your *if* sentences. In some sentences use *when* or *whenever* instead of *if.* Examples: *If she is tired, he brings her breakfast in bed. Whenever he sees her, he smiles.*

2 Talking politics

If with something that is possible
(*if* + present simple, + *will*/modal)

Work as a class. Talk about the things that your government(s) are planning to do. Say what will happen if they do them. Examples: *If they help the car industry, there will be more jobs. If they borrow more, there may be more inflation.*

Here are some ideas to help you. Use them and your own ideas to make *if* sentences for possibility using *if* + present simple, and *will* or a modal verb like *may, might* or *could*.

Ideas

improve the motorway between . . . and . . .
do more for trade between . . . and . . .

export more . . .	help the . . . industry
pass a law about . . .	build more houses
build better prisons	import less . . .
develop the . . . industry	increase/reduce taxes

3 Amazing luck

If with something that is unlikely
(*if* + past simple, + *would*)

1 Work in pairs. Say what you would do if you won a million pounds. Use *if* + past simple and *would,* like this: *If I won a million pounds, I would go round the world.*

2 Work as a class. Tell the class what you would do. List some of the suggestions that other people in the class make.

B Grammar guide

1	**Something that is always true** ***If* + present simple, + present simple**	■ Use *if* with two present simple verbs to say what always happens. *If I* ***eat*** *too much, I* ***get*** *fat.* The *if* can usually be replaced by *when* or *whenever.* *When I* ***eat*** *too much, I* ***get*** *fat.* ■ You can also use the present progressive or present perfect in the *if* clause. *If you* ***are travelling to*** *Liverpool, you* ***change*** *at London.* *If you* ***have come*** *from Paris,* ***collect*** *your baggage now.*
2	**Something that is possible** ***If* + present simple, + *will***	Use *if* + present simple and the future with *will* to talk about something that may possibly happen (but may not happen). (This is sometimes called Conditional 1.) *I'**ll** give it to Mary if I* ***see*** *her.* OR *If I* ***see*** *Mary, I'**ll** give it to her.* (= It is possible that I will see Mary and if I do, I will definitely give it to her.) *If you* ***work*** *hard, you'**ll** pass the exam.* (= It is possible that you will work hard and if you do, you will definitely pass the exam.)
3	**Something that is not true in the present, or unlikely in the future** ***If* + past simple, + *would***	Use *if* + past simple and *would* to talk about something that is not true now or that you think is unlikely to happen in the future. (This is sometimes called Conditional 2.) *If I* ***had*** *a lot of money, I* ***would*** *spend it all on you.* (present) (= I don't have a lot of money; I am imagining that I do.) *If the world* ***ended*** *tomorrow, I* ***wouldn't*** *care.* (future) (= It is unlikely that the world will end tomorow; I am imagining that it might.)
4	**Something that is imaginary in the past** ***If* + past perfect, + *would have***	Use *if* + past perfect and *would have* to talk about something that was possible but which didn't happen. (This is sometimes called Conditional 3.) *If I* ***had gone*** *to Italy last year, I* ***would have*** *visited you.* (But I did not go to Italy, so I did not visit you.) *I would have bought some food if I had thought of it.* (But I didn't think of it, so I didn't buy any food.) *If had known that you had all that food, I wouldn't have brought any.* (But I didn't know, so I did buy some.)
5	***If* with modals**	You can use modal verbs with all four types of *if* sentence (types 1–4 above). ■ Always true: *If I understand it, I* ***can*** *learn it.* ■ Possible: *You* ***must*** *give it to Jane if you see her.* ■ Not true or unlikely (present or future time): *I* ***could*** *help Maria more if she came to lessons more often.* *If John lost weight, he* ***could*** *ride that little pony.* ■ Imaginary (past time): *If John had gone to Italy last year, he* ***could have*** *visited you.*

C Activities

1 Hamlet

If imaginary in past time

1 Work as a class. Here is the story of Hamlet. Use it to help you make *if* sentences from the flowchart. Make an *if* sentence from each box in the flowchart. Examples: *If Hamlet's father hadn't died, Gertrude would not have remarried. If Gertrude hadn't remarried . . .*

The story of Hamlet
Hamlet was the Prince of Denmark. His father died and his mother, Gertrude, soon married his uncle Claudius. Because Claudius had married the Queen, he became King of Denmark. The ghost of Hamlet's father comes to Hamlet and says that Claudius killed him. At first Hamlet wants to kill his uncle Claudius. But he is very indecisive and doesn't do it. He tells some actors to act out the murder of his father. The actors act out the murder and everyone can see from Claudius's face that he really is the murderer. But still Hamlet does nothing. Hamlet is losing interest in his girlfriend Ophelia. Ophelia's father Polonius is a bit of a fool who keeps giving everybody advice they do not want. One day Hamlet is talking to Gertrude and he hears a noise behind a curtain. He takes out his sword and kills the man behind the curtain. It is Polonius. Ophelia goes mad. Hamlet gets into a swordfight with Laertes, Ophelia's brother. During the swordfight Hamlet is killed.

Flowchart

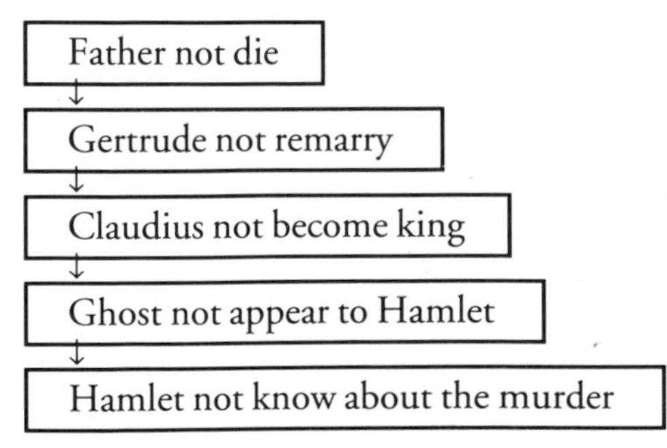

2 Work in pairs. Continue the story of Hamlet by making *if* sentences with the past perfect and *would have* or *might have* from the flowchart.

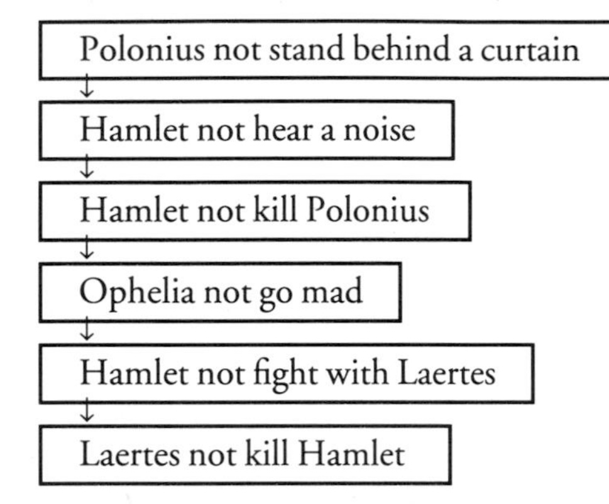

2 Decisions

If for something that is possible

1 Work as a class. At one point in the Hamlet story, Hamlet is deciding whether or not to kill Claudius. Make affirmative and negative *if* sentences about the situation. Examples: *If Hamlet kills Claudius he might go to prison. If Hamlet doesn't kill Claudius he'll never be King of Denmark.*

2 Work in pairs. Think of other people in well-known stories and make *if* sentences at the point in the story where they have to make a decision. Use stories you know, or the ideas below.

Ideas
Cinderella deciding whether or not to go to the ball.
Cinderella deciding whether or not to marry the prince. (Activity note 7, page 138)
King Lear deciding whether or not to give away all his money and power. (Unit 29, page 122)

D Accuracy practice

1 **Raymond is talking to his doctor. Match the half sentences 1 to 5 with the half sentences (a) to (e) to make five correct sentences.**

1 If I don't get better, . . .
2 Whenever I go up the stairs quickly . . .
3 If I went to bed late every night, . . .
4 When I try to lift anything . . .
5 If I eat fried or rich food, . . .

a it is always too heavy for me.
b I have to stop half-way up and have a rest.
c I would understand why I'm always tired.
d I feel sick.
e I'll have to stop going to work.

2 **Complete these sentences about an office using the verbs in brackets and *will* or *would* where necessary. More than one answer is sometimes possible.**

1 If Mr Bowen ____ (call back), tell him that I ____ (fax) the letter to him.
2 I ____ (buy) a bigger office block if I ____ (own) Mr Bowen's company. But I don't own it.
3 The goods are here. If we ____ (send) them tomorrow they ____ (arrive) early next week. But if we ____ (send) them today, they ____ (get) there on Monday.
4 The sales staff ____ (earn) more if we ____ (pay) them a bonus every time they ____ (make) a large sale, but we don't do that.
5 When the buyer from Derhams ____ (phone), Mr Prothero ____ (speak) to him.
6 If Mr Rogerson ____ (ask) you, please tell him that I ____ (not/be) there until tomorrow.
7 If you ____ (finish) typing those letters, Jim, please ____ (not/sit) there doing nothing.
8 We ____ (use) the computer more if we ____ (not/have) such an old one.

3 **These sentences are about an old man's regrets as he looks back on his life. Make sentences with *if* + past perfect, + *would have* or *wouldn't have.***

Example: (1) *If I hadn't been too shy to talk to the other children at school, I would have learned to get on with people.*

1 At school I was too shy to talk to the other children and so I never learned to get on with people.
2 At primary school I never learned to do maths and so I didn't take jobs that used numbers.
3 At secondary school I did not work hard and so I did not pass my examinations.
4 I never learned to dance at the youth club and so I was shy with girls.
5 I never learned to speak clearly at job interviews and so I never did well at them.
6 At the office I never worked hard and so I never got promotion.

21

Phrasal verbs II: by adverb (*down*, *in*, *off*, *out*, *up* etc.)

A Starting activities

1 Brainstorming

Learning phrasal verbs

Work as a class. List all the phrasal verbs that people in the class can think of with the adverb particles *down*, *in*, *off*, *out* and *up*.

When you have finished, look at Activity note 32 on page 145.

2 I must dash off

Phrasal verbs with *off*

Work in pairs. This activity is to help you learn some more phrasal verbs. Put the phrasal verbs in the sentences below (a–i) into one of these groups. (One of the phrasal verbs does not fit into any of the groups.)

Groups

Group 1: *off* for 'moving away' or 'separation'
Group 2: *off* for 'stopping' (electricity, water, arrangements, activities)
Group 3: *off* for 'going to sleep'
Group 4: *off* for 'not at work'

Sentences

a I must dash off. I'm in a hurry.
b Grandad's dropped off to sleep in the armchair.
c I'm taking the morning off work to go to the dentist's.
d Would you like me to drop you off at the station?
e They stole the car and drove off before I could get a good look at them.
f I get off work at five-thirty. I could meet you then.
g George dozed off on the bus and missed his stop.
h The cooker's gone off. There must be a power cut.
i Ugh! Just smell that milk. It's gone off.

When you have finished, look at Activity note 28 on page 144.

3 He gave up hope

Phrasal verbs with *up*

Work in pairs, A and B. Look at Activity note 20 on page 141, which has a list of phrasal verbs with *up*.
Person A: Find all the phrasal verbs that mean 'getting bigger', or 'more' in some way.
Example: *Blow up this balloon for me, please.*
Person B: Find all the phrasal verbs that mean 'stopping' or 'finishing' or 'completing an action'.
Example: *I gave up smoking last year.*
Compare your answers.

When you have finished, look at Activity note 62 on page 156.

4 Phrasal verb game

Remembering phrasal verbs

The class is in two teams. Someone from one team says a phrasal verb with the adverb particle *down*, *in*, *off*, *out* or *up*. The other team gets a point for putting it into a correct sentence. The first team to get five points wins. You can read the Grammar guide first, if you like. Play the game with this book closed.

B Grammar guide

One of the problems with learning phrasal verbs is that there are a lot of them. Putting them into groups helps you to remember them.

1 *down*

- *down* for 'lower' or 'less':
  cool down (people, food, machines)
  go down (prices)
  turn down (radio, television)
  cut down (= reduce)
  slow down (= go at a lower speed)
  calm down (= be less agitated)
- *down* for 'failure':
  break down (machines)
  close down (factory, shop)

2 *in*

in for 'inside', 'indoors' or 'in an inward direction':
check in (at a hotel)
call/drop in (on someone)
get in (planes, trains)
let someone in
lie/sleep in (= stay in bed)
move in (with someone or to a new house)
plug in (television, video etc.)

3 *off*

- *off* for 'moving away' or 'separation':
  run/dash/hurry/rush off
  take off (aeroplanes)
  drive off (cars or motorcycles)
  shave off (beard or moustache)
  take off (clothes)
  send something off (= post)
  drop someone off (take someone somewhere by car then continue your journey)
- *off* for 'stopping' (electricity, water, arrangements, activities):
  turn off (taps)
  switch off (lights)
  call off (meetings)
  break off (relationships)
  ring off (after a phone conversation)
  put off (= do later)
  finish off (= complete)

4 *out*

- *out* for 'outside, outdoors' or 'in an outward direction':
  stay out (= get home late)
  pop out (= leave for a short time)
  eat out (in a restaurant)
  have something out (e.g. a tooth or your appendix)
  let clothes out (= make them bigger)
- *out* when something is 'finished':
  sell out of (= sell all of something)
  run out (e.g. passports = expire)
  put out (fire, cigarette)
  run out of (= have none left)
  rub out (words etc. on the board)
  wipe out (= destroy completely)
  wash/rub out (a stain)

5 *up*

- *up* for 'getting bigger' or 'more' in some way:
  bring up (children)
  go up (prices)
  grow up (children)
  put up (prices, taxes)
  turn up (radio, television)
  warm up (= get warmer)
- *up* for 'into pieces':
  cut/slice/chop up
  break/split up (marriage or relationship)
- *up* for 'finished':
  give up (smoking)

C Activities

1 Story time

Building and using phrasal verbs

1. Work in pairs or groups. Copy out the three phrasal verb grids below. Tick every possible verb + adverb particle combination (like *give back* in grid 1) and put a cross against combinations which are not possible (like ~~*break on*~~) in grid 2. If a possible verb + adverb particle combination is new to you, ask your partner or someone in your group to put it into a sentence.
   Example (from grid 1): *give off. These eggs are giving off a funny smell.*

Grid 1	give	put	send	pull
back	✓			
off				
down				
over				

Grid 2	break	take	fall	drive
on	×			
up				
in				
away				

Grid 3	get	let	go	tear
through	✓			
out				
up				
about				

   When you have finished, look at Activity note 63 on page 156.

2. As a class choose a story, fable or myth that everybody knows. Outline the story briefly as a class, as quickly as you can, making sure you know all the most important vocabulary.

3. In pairs or groups, tell or write the story in detail, putting in as many phrasal verbs from the three grids as you naturally can.

2 English in situations

Using phrasal verbs with *down, in, on, up, off, out*

1. Work in pairs or groups. Write down four phrasal verbs. Each of the four phrasal verbs must have one of the adverb particles *down, in, on, up, off* or *out.* Give the piece of paper with the four phrasal verbs on it to another pair or group.

2. Have a conversation using the four phrasal verbs you were given as if you were in one of the situations below. If you are working in pairs use one of the situations for pairs. If you are working in groups use one of the situations for groups.

Situations for pairs

a. One of you is buying either furniture, or a new hi-fi or some stereo equipment, or a new car or motorbike. The other person is the shop assistant.
b. You have just taken your boss out to dinner. At the end of a three-course meal you realize you have no money, no chequebook, no credit cards and no means of identification on you. The other person is the manager of the restaurant.
c. You and the other person are at a bus stop waiting for a bus. You and the other person like the look of each other and want to get to know each other.
d. Your car has just run out of petrol. The other person stops to ask what is wrong.

Situations for groups

a. Tell the other members of the group the best or worst thing that ever happened to you in another country.
b. You are all passengers on a train which stops in the middle of a tunnel. Silence. Darkness. React to the situation. Talk to the other people in the group.

D Accuracy practice

1 Complete these sentences with a phrasal verb that includes one of the adverbs and one of the verbs below:
adverbs: *down, in, out, up*
verbs: *turn, put, slow, let, have, go, drop, grow, warm, plug.*

1 The dentist says John will have to ____ two teeth ____ .
2 Please ____ ____ for a cup of coffee whenever you are passing.
3 Would you ____ the television ____ , please. It's very loud.
4 Videos are cheaper now. Prices have actually ____ ____ since the 1980s.
5 He could play the guitar when he was six. I think he's going to be musical when he ____ ____.
6 ____ ____ ! You are driving much too fast!
7 Smoking isn't allowed in here. Please ____ that cigarette ____ .
8 You must be very cold. Sit by the fire and ____ ____.
9 There's someone at the door. Can you ____ them ____ , please?
10 Look, there's the plug on the floor. You haven't ____ the television ____.

2 Complete the sentences with a phrasal verb with the particle *off*.

1 The Director is ill, so the meeting can't take place.
We will have to ____ it ____ .
2 You don't need to catch a bus.
I'll ____ you ____ on my way to work.
3 I didn't recognize you. Where's your moustache?
When did you ____ it ____ ?
4 I was talking to Jonathan on the phone.
The minute I ____ ____, I thought of something else I wanted to say.

3 Replace the one-word verbs in the dialogue which are printed in *italic* with phrasal verbs. Maria and Julia work together in the Finance Department of a company.

MARIA My visa (1) *expires* on Tuesday so I can't (2) *postpone* getting it renewed any longer.
JULIA You can just (3) *post* it to the Immigration Office, can't you?
MARIA No, it's too late for that. I'll have to (4) *hurry* to the office myself today. I can (5) *finish* work at four if I do these accounts quickly. Oh, and some time I must (6) *go* to the shop for some cigarettes. The little newsagent's on the corner had (7) *sold* all the ones I smoke.
JULIA Maria, (8) *relax*, please. I thought you had (9) *stopped* smoking. When did you start again?
MARIA This morning. Because I'm so worried about my visa.

22

Adverbs of manner, time and place

A Starting activities

1 You said that passionately

Adverbs of manner

Work in pairs. Take it in turns to choose one of the quotations from the list below and say it in the manner of one of the adverbs from the list of adverbs below. For example, say it angrily or bitterly. Your partner has to guess which adverb it is. Guess like this: *You said that passionately.*

Quotations
The love of money is the root of all evil. (The Bible)
It's so difficult to know what the people we love really need. (Ugo Betti)
Friendship often ends in love; but love in friendship – never. (Charles Caleb Colton)
A teacher is better than two books. (German proverb)
It is better to lose the saddle than the horse. (Italian proverb)

Adverbs: bitterly, calmly, cheerfully, confidently, excitedly, furiously, gloomily, gratefully, helplessly, impatiently, miserably, nervously, passionately, proudly

2 A sad occasion

Adverbs and adverbials of time

1 Notice the position of the adverbs and adverbial phrases (adverbials) in these sentences:
John **still** lives in New York. (before the verb)
Jane hasn't finished her meal **yet**. (at the end of the sentence)
I have **already** written to Mark. (before the verb)
In her career she visited lots of countries. OR
She visited lots of countries **during her twenties**. (at the beginning or end of the sentence)

2 Work in pairs. Imagine that after a long, happy and successful life your teacher has died, at the age of 94. Write sentences for a newspaper obituary about her or him. The obituary should be about your teacher's life, work and successes. Each sentence must have one of the adverbs or adverbials of time below in it. Example: *His wife still lives at their old home.*

Adverbs of time: *still, yet, already*
Adverbials of time: *throughout his life/childhood, during every summer, since leaving university, for ten years, in his twenties*

3 Work as a class. Put some of your sentences together to make a one-paragraph obituary for your teacher to go in the local newspaper.

3 Sorting them out

Adverbs of manner, time and place

Work as a class. Use the Grammar guide to help you, if you need to.

1 Which of these are not adverbs?
badly, beautiful, yesterday, table, here, fast, everywhere, sat

2 Which of these are adverbs of manner, which are adverbs of time and which are adverbs of place?
yet, anywhere, recently, nastily, fast, eventually, upstairs

When you have finished, look at Activity note 68 on page 159.

B Grammar guide

1 Adverbs of manner, time and place

- Adverbs tell you more about an action. Adverbs of manner, time and place are used with verbs and tell you how, when or where the action happened.
  The team played ***badly.*** (Adverb of manner. How did they play?)
  The team played ***yesterday.*** (Adverb of time. When did they play?)
  The team played ***nearby.*** (Adverb of place. Where did they play?)

2 Adverbs of manner

You can often form adverbs of manner by adding *-ly* to the adjective, but there are sometimes spelling changes. For example: *happy* → *happily* (and *easily, angrily*); *true* → *truly*; *sensible* → *sensibly* (and *comfortably, reasonably*); *automatic* → *automatically.*
Some useful adverbs of manner which do not end in *-ly* are *hard, fast* and *well.*
Gillian hit the ball hard.

3 Adverbs and adverbials of time

- Examples are: *now, yesterday, still, yet, already, early, late, soon, recently, lately* (= recently).
  Use *still* when the action is continuing. It is often used when you are surprised that something is taking so long.
  Are you still writing that letter? You started an hour ago.
  Yet is used in questions or negative sentences, and comes at the end of the sentence. Use it to talk about something that is expected.
  We asked Peter to come at three, but he isn't here yet and it's three-thirty.
  Use *already* to say that something has happened early.
  I got there on time but the train had already gone.
- The prepositions *throughout, during, in, for* and *since* can be used in adverbial phrases. They are used like adverbs to talk about periods of time.
  We use *throughout* to mean 'right through a period of time'.
  It rained throughout July. (It didn't stop raining in July.)
  We use *during* or *throughout* when we are talking about an activity (e.g. a journey) which happened over a period of time.
  She read magazines during/throughout the journey.
  We use *in* or *during* to mean 'at some point or points in a period'.
  It rained three times in/during July.
  Use *for* to say how long something lasted.
  I have lived here for five years.
  Use *since* to say when something started.
  I've known her since 1990.

4 Adverbs and adverbials of place

Some phrases starting with a preposition can be adverbials of place, for example, *on the right.* Examples of adverbs and adverbials of place are: *here, below, upstairs, next door, close to, anywhere, in the corner* (of a room), *on the corner* (of a street), *everywhere, at home.*
There were flies everywhere. It was horrible.

C Activities

1 You can put your sleeping bag on the sofa

Adverbs and adverbials of place

1 Work as a class. Make sure you understand this situation. At the end of a holiday A cannot get home. (Why not? Bad weather? A strike?) An old friend, B, lives in the town where A spent his or her holiday, so A decides to visit B. A arrives at B's flat unexpectedly with two big cases, a rucksack and a sleeping bag. (What is in the cases, and the rucksack?) A wants to stay with B for a while.

2 Work in pairs. You are both A. Make as many questions as you can about where you can sleep, and where you can put all the things you have brought with you. Each question must have an adverb or adverbial of place in it. Example: *Can I put my clothes in your cupboard, please?*

3 Now you are both B. Make as many sentences as you can telling A where everything is that A might need, and making any necessary arrangements for A's stay. Each sentence must have an adverb or adverbial of place in it. Examples: *There's a big washing machine for all the flats in the basement. You can put your sleeping bag on the sofa.*

2 Cinderella cried noisily

Adverbs of manner

1 Work in pairs or groups. Choose one of the stories below and make it more interesting by putting in three or more adverbs of manner. Use the list of adverbs of manner below to help you but use adverbs that are not on the list, if you want to. Change the stories if necessary, so that as many adverbs as possible will fit in naturally.

Stories: Cinderella (Activity note 7, page 138), David and Goliath (Unit 26, page 110), Hamlet (Unit 20, page 86)

Adverbs of manner: *accidentally, angrily, badly, carefully, carelessly, clumsily, dangerously, deliberately, easily, excitedly, fiercely, firmly, hastily, honestly, loudly, noisily, patiently, peacefully, perfectly, politely, quietly, roughly, rudely, secretly, sensibly, silently, strangely, thoroughly, truthfully, warmly*

2 Work as a class. Tell your story to the class with the adverbs in it. Listen to other people in the class's stories and suggest adverbs which could have been put in that were not.

3 Adverb pairs

Adverbs of manner

1 Work as a class. Describe imaginary people, using pairs of the adverbs of manner list from Activity 2 that go together and a suitable verb. Pair off as many of the adverbs on the list as you can. Example: *He was dressed badly and carelessly.*

2 Work as a class. Can you think of adverbs that are not on the list to make a pair with any unpaired adverbs from Activity 2? Try making adverbs of manner by adding *-ly* to adjectives, like this: *calm* (adjective), *calmly* (adverb).

D Accuracy practice

1 Complete the sentences using these adverbs of time.

still, yet, already, late, soon, lately

1 I'm afraid you are too late. I've ____ sold the car that was advertised in the paper.
2 There's ____ some cake left. Would you like another piece?
3 Haven't you finished with that hammer ____ ?
4 Gavin is not here yet but we are expecting him ____ . He's never late.
5 I don't know what's wrong, but he's been in a bad mood ____ .
6 Everybody else was here on time but Sarah always arrives ____ . She usually keeps everyone waiting.

2 Complete the sentences using these adverbials of time.

during (×2), *for, throughout, since*

1 The phone rang twice ____ the night.
2 The detective followed the suspect ____ the night. The detective didn't lose sight of him until the morning.
3 There was a bad storm ____ the flight so we had to land at the nearest airport.
4 I only slept ____ four hours last night.
5 ____ last week I have slept really well every night.

3 Choose one word from each box to make an adverbial of place which completes the sentence.

on (×3) *in* *outside*

the corner *the door* *the top shelf* *the left* *the fridge*

1 Put the milk ____ to keep it cold.
2 You can leave those tins of food ____ of the cupboard.
3 Can you get us both a meal from the take-away ____ ?
4 Go down this corridor to the last door ____ . That's the bathroom.
5 Could you stand your bike up ____ , please?

4 Complete the text using these adverbs of manner.

honestly, deliberately, miserably, happily, quietly, excitedly, carelessly

He ran up to us on the beach [1]____ , out of breath, his eyes wild. He was obviously bringing some bad news. A big lorry had crashed into our house and had done a lot of damage. Richard kept saying that the driver had not done it [2]____ , as if that helped us at all. It seems that the lorry had been parked [3]____ at the top of the hill and some children had taken the handbrake off. We sat there [4]____ , our holiday ruined and both of us close to tears. Then Richard calmed down. 'I'm doing all I can,' he said [5]____ . 'I've told you [6]____ that there is a lot of damage but I'll do what I can to help.' I started to feel sorry for myself. Our first holiday for years and Janice and I had been sitting on the beach so [7]____ before Richard appeared.

The passive

A Starting activities

1 Life in prison

Present simple passive

Work in pairs. Describe the lives of prisoners in a prison. Use present simple passive sentences and use the list of verbs and the pictures below to give you ideas.
Example: *They are woken by an alarm at 6.30 a.m.*

Verbs: *wake, allow, take, teach, count, lead, watch, bring, give*

1 allow . . . play games

2 take . . . see visitors

3 teach . . . repair cars

2 MacBurger's delicious burgers

Present progressive passive

Work in pairs. Take it in turns to be a waiter at MacBurger's restaurant. Your partner is the cook. Customers keep complaining that the food is taking a long time to arrive. The cook uses present progressive passive sentences to say what is happening to the food. Use the foods and verbs below to help you. Example:

WAITER *Where's the ice-cream?*
COOK *It's (just) being prepared.*

Food: chips, burgers, coffee, tea, coke, eggs, beans, apple pie, ice-cream, milkshakes

Verbs: *prepare, fry, boil, grill, make, pour, put* (on the tray), *take out* (of the oven), *finish, cook, serve, freeze, cut, heat up*

3 Active or passive?

When to use the active and the passive

Work as a class. Which in the pairs of sentences below is more natural, the active or the passive?

1 A: What do the Marconi family eat?
B: They eat a lot of Italian food. (ACTIVE)
B: A lot of Italian food is eaten by them. (PASSIVE)

2 On a notice
ACTIVE We will prosecute trespassers.
PASSIVE Trespassers will be prosecuted.

3 A: Where's your car?
B: The garage is servicing it. (ACTIVE)
B: It's being serviced. (PASSIVE)

When you have finished, look at Activity note 60 on page 155.

B Grammar guide

1 The form of the passive

- The passive is formed by *be* and the past participle.

Simple present	*is/are* + past participle: *Smoking is not allowed.*
Present progressive	*is/are being* + past participle: *Dinner is being served.*
Simple past	*was/were* + past participle: *He was killed.*
Past progressive	*was/were being* + past participle: *It was being repaired.*
Present perfect	*has/have been* + past participle: *They've been hurt.*
Past perfect	*had been* + past participle: *It had already been done.*
Future	*will be* + past participle: *It will be built soon.*
	is going to be + past participle: *It is going to be built soon.*

- We can use *by* or *with* in passive sentences before an agent (someone who does the action), an instrument (what the action is done with) and a material (what something is made of).

Agent	*'Hamlet' was written* ***by*** *Shakespeare.*
Instrument	*He was killed* ***with*** *a knife.*
	The building was hit ***by*** *lightning.*
Material	*The best coffee is made* ***with*** *good coffee beans.*

2 The use of the passive

Use the passive when it is not important who or what did the action, or when we don't know who or what did the action.
This church was built in 1688. (The agent is not important.)
My car has been stolen. (The agent is unknown.)
The passive is used in:

- Formal notices: *Passengers are requested not to smoke until the aircraft stops.*
- Newspapers: *A man is being questioned about the robbery.*
- Processes in science or engineering: *The engine is cooled by air, not water.*

3 Verbs with the passive

Many active verbs have no passive because the agent is usually known and important. For example: *escape, fit, get, have, let, like, suit, survive.*
These shoes don't suit me. (no passive is possible)
He escaped from prison. (no passive is possible)
They got married last week. (no passive is possible)
On the other hand, these verbs are passive, not active:
I was born in Oxford. (always passive and always past tense)
He's said to be a great writer. (= people say he is)

4 Sentence structures with the passive

- After modals (including *will*) use *be* + past participle.
  This problem can be solved.
  To talk about the past, with a modal, use *have been* + past participle.
  The baby should have been fed hours ago.
- We can use the passive + infinitive + object with these verbs: *advise, believe, expect, feel, forbid, mean, order, report, request, require, say, teach, understand.*
  I was taught to use the passive at school.
- We often use *it* as the subject of these verbs in the passive: *agree, announce, discover, expect, hope, suggest.*
  It was agreed that we would arrive at six.

C Activities

1 The kidnapping of Horace Boot

Passive with past tenses

1 Work in pairs or groups. Millionaire Horace Boot, aged 68, was kidnapped and a ransom was demanded from his nephew Clyde. Write between ten and fifteen passive sentences about what happened from when Horace Boot was kidnapped, to when the kidnappers were caught by the police. Use the main events below to help you.

Main events

- The kidnapping (How was he kidnapped? Where was he taken? What was he given to eat and drink? What was he allowed to do?)
- The paying of the ransom (What was Clyde told to do? How much was he asked to pay?)
- The police hunt (The police were told. By whom? A member of the kidnap gang was seen. By whom? Where was the money left? Where was Horace released? How were the gang arrested?)

2 Work as a class. You are making a film of the Horace Boot kidnap story. Take the best suggestions from everybody in the class for the main events and plan the film. (Which stars do you want in it?) Use passive sentences only where it is natural to do so.

2 Moving

Past simple and present perfect passive and modals (*may/might/could*)

1 Work in pairs or small groups. You are moving to a new flat. Quickly list at least twenty items that will be moved on the removal van. Make sure that you include furniture, personal possessions, children's toys, clothes.

2 When you get to the new flat everything has been lost or damaged in some way. Take it in turns to ask each other about everything on the list. Answer with a past or present perfect passive sentence if you are sure what has happened to the item. Answer with a present perfect passive with modal *may/might/could* if you are not sure. There are verbs below to give you ideas. Examples:
A: *Where's the . . .?/What's happened to the . . .?*
B: *It was dropped down the stairs./It's been left behind./It may have been left behind.*

Verbs: *drop, smash, break, tear, lose, leave behind, damage, forget, take* (to the wrong flat, for example), *run over, squash*

3 Mad machines

Passive, all tenses

1 Work in pairs or small groups. Design and draw a 'mad machine'; for example, a machine for making sunshine, a machine for making money out of banana skins, a machine for making people happy or a machine for punishing people you do not like.

2 Explain how your machine works to another pair or group or to the whole class. Use the ideas below to help you but use the passive only where it seems natural to do so.

Ideas

The engine is started from here.
While the people are being strapped in . . .
When all the juice has been squeezed out . . .
When this button is pressed . . .
A weight is released.
When this lever is pulled . . .
Coins are put in the slot here, and then . . .

D Accuracy practice

1 Make these sentences passive ONLY where possible.

1 Those shoes really suit you.
2 We export eighty per cent of what we produce.
3 Sharon and Jim survived a night on the mountain in winter.
4 We expect trainee pilots to land an aircraft after twenty hours of instruction.
5 We will send you the papers immediately.
6 Three prisoners escaped from the prison during the night.
7 One moment, please. The waiter is just adding up your bill.
8 Mick's got a new motorbike.
9 By the time I arrived, someone had already opened all your letters.

2 Make all these sentences passive. Don't use phrases with *by* or *with*.

1 The firm promised us our money back.
We ______________
2 The travel agent told them that the hotel was near the sea.
They ______________
3 The other children were always calling Harriet stupid.
Harriet ______________
4 The box office had sold the last tickets just before we got there.
The last tickets ______________
5 Passport control should have stopped her.
She ______________

3 Write out these passive sentences in full.

1 If you/required/for an interview, you/notified/by letter tomorrow.
2 He was an old man. His trousers/held up/with a safety pin/which/pinned/to his shirt.
3 Parcels cannot/sent/through the post tied up with string.
4 The car/hit/by falling rocks as we drove along the valley.
5 The roof of this church/has just/repaired/with local wood.

4 Put the verb in brackets into the correct passive tense in this report.

Three men [1]____ (want) by the police in connection with a robbery at a petrol station. The cashier [2]____ (hold up) and [3]____ (threaten) with a knife. While the money [4]____ (steal) the cashier [5]____ (tie up) by one of the men. Some car parts [6]____ (also/steal), but the cashier's wallet [7]____ (not/take). The men escaped in a blue Volvo car which police believe [8]____ (use) in other robberies.

5 Put the verbs in brackets into the correct passive tense to complete this description of the production of baked beans.

The tomato purée [1]____ (send) here from Italy and Greece in the form of a concentrate. It [2]____ (dilute) with ordinary water and then sugar, spices, and starch [3]____ (add). When they [4]____ (add), it [5]____ (mix) together and [6]____ (heat). The sauce must [7]____ (heat) before it reaches the production line so that the beans can [8]____ (add) to it.

24

Future progressive (*he will be working*) and future perfect (*he will have worked*)

A Starting activities

1 This time next week

Future progressive and future perfect

1 Read the conversation between Sandra and Karen and make sure you understand it. If you want to, you can read it aloud in pairs.

SANDRA This time tomorrow I'll be lying on a beach in the sun.
KAREN Really. I'll be working as usual.
SANDRA Yes, I'll be staying at the Ritz, in my usual room.
KAREN Good, good. I'll be thinking of you. Can we talk about these letters? I . . .
SANDRA I'll be meeting the usual crowd. Sometimes I wish *all* my friends weren't rock stars.
KAREN Sandra, will you have typed these letters before you go?
SANDRA Letters? What letters? Oh, those! Yes, yes. I'll be having dinner at one of the best restaurants in the world tomorrow evening.
KAREN Good.
SANDRA And I'll be going up in a helicopter the next day.
KAREN Sandra, about the work . . .
SANDRA Don't worry about the work, Karen. I'll have finished it all by three o'clock.
KAREN Will you? Look at it all. You won't have done all that by three o'clock. What are you typing at the moment?
SANDRA This . . .? Oh, it's a letter to one of my friends. He's a rock star. Can you post it for me?

2 Work in the same pairs. Underline all the future progressive sentences (*will* + *be* + the *-ing* form) and all the future perfect sentences (*will* + *have* + past participle) in the dialogue.

When you have finished, look at Activity note 14 on page 140.

2 Let's go somewhere else

Future perfect

1 As a class, plan a timetable for moving the school where you are learning English to the next town. Start like this:

Monday 9.00 a.m. *put the tables and chairs outside*
Monday 9.30 a.m. *put the tables and chairs in the removal van*
Monday 10.00 a.m. . . .

2 In pairs make future perfect sentences from your timetable. Start like this: *By 9.30 a.m. we will have put the tables and chairs outside. By 10.00 a.m. we will have put . . .*

B Grammar guide

1 Future progressive

The future progressive is formed with *will* + *be* + the *-ing* form.
He will be working on his new book.
He won't be coming next week.
Will she be staying with the firm until next year?
We use the future PROGRESSive whenever something will be happening (it will be in PROGRESS) in the future.

- Use the future progressive to talk about what you will be doing at a definite time in the future.
  This time tomorrow I'll be lying on a beach in the sun.
  I'll be leaving here at three o'clock.
- Use the future progressive when you want to describe the length of time into the future that something will continue for.
  She'll be working here for another five years.
- You can also use the future progressive as a polite way of asking about someone's plans.
  Will you be using the car next week? (This means 'I would like to use the car but it is OK if you want it.')

NOTE There is a future progressive with *going to* (*going to* + *be* + the *-ing* form). In nearly all cases you can use it instead of the future progressive with *will.*
She's going to be working here for another five years.

2 Future perfect

The future perfect is formed with *will* + *have* + the past participle.
He will have worked.
We won't have finished.
Will they have arrived?

- Use the future perfect to talk about something which will be completed before a definite time or event in the future.
  They'll have delivered the paint by tomorrow.
  By the time you read this I'll have finished all my work.
- *By* or *before* are often used with the future perfect in positive sentences.
  She'll have written the book before the baby is born.
  Until with a specific time is often used with the future perfect in negative sentences.
  They won't have finished painting until Tuesday.

C Activities

1 A sponsored activity for charity

Future progressive

1 Work in pairs or small groups. You want to raise money for charity. (Which charity?) To do this, you are planning a sponsored activity. For example, you can plan to push a bed from one end of your country or region to the other. Sponsors will pay a certain amount to your charity for every kilometre that you push the bed. Decide what your sponsored activity is. Make future progressive sentences (positive and negative) about your activity. You will need the sentences in 2. Examples: *Six of us will be taking it in turns to push the bed. We won't be taking any breaks, except at night.*

2 Work with another pair (or another small group). Each pair (or small group) takes it in turns to be the possible sponsor. Using your future progressive sentences, describe your activity to the possible sponsor. The possible sponsor asks questions about the other pair or group's activity, using the future progressive, like this: *Will anybody be lying in the bed, while you push it?* Answer all the possible sponsor's questions about your activity.

2 What I will have done

Future perfect

1 Work on your own. Talk to as many people in the class as possible about what they think they will have done by the time they are forty (or sixty). Ask future perfect questions and remember or write down the answers. Examples: *What do you think you will have done by the time you are forty? Do you think you will have got married by the time you are forty?* Answer other people's questions.

2 Tell the class the information you found out, using future perfect positive and negative sentences, like this: *Maria will have opened a restaurant. Peter won't have got married.*

3 Mountain climbing

Future progressive and future perfect

1 Work in pairs. Write a dialogue together. The dialogue is about your preparations and plans to climb the highest mountain in your country next summer. The dialogue should contain as many future progressive and future perfect sentences as is naturally possible. Use the vocabulary about mountain climbing below to help you. Your written dialogue should start like this:

A: *When will you have bought all the equipment we'll need?*

B: *Well, by the end of the month I . . .*

Use the future perfect for:

- travel and other arrangements you will have made and equipment you will have bought by a definite time in the future. *By the end of this month I will have arranged transport for our equipment.*
- calculating how long the food and water will last. *By the time we have been on the mountain ten days we will have used half of the dried food.*

Use the future progressive for:

- anticipating problems. *We'll be spending a lot of time very high up so we will need oxygen.*

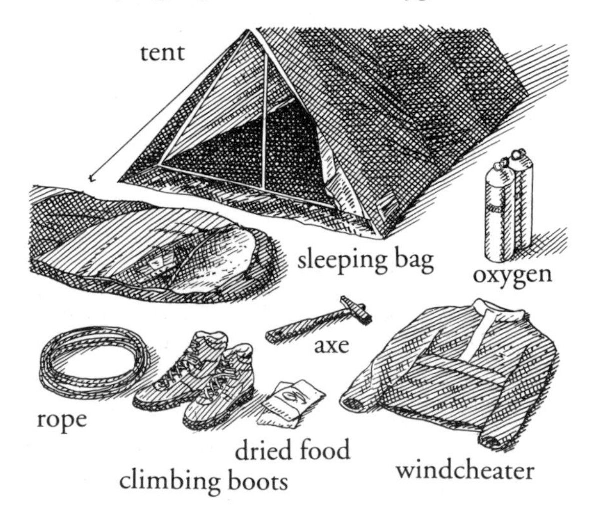

2 In the same pairs, read your dialogue to the class. List some future perfect and future progressive sentences from other people's dialogues.

D Accuracy practice

1 **Tina Bradshaw is the Managing Director of a computer company. Here are some notes from her business diary for Monday morning.**

1	8.00	talk to Mrs Lewis about the Compact order
2	8.30	breakfast with the architect – discuss the new building
3	9.15	telephone Tom in New York to wish him a Happy Birthday
4	9.30	dictate letters
5	10.00	have a meeting with J and M about the Compact order
6	11.00	talk to the new trainees
7	11.30	write a report of the J and M meeting
8	12.30	lunch with the new Sales Manager

On the Friday before, the Personnel Manager telephoned Miss Bradshaw's secretary. He wanted to have a meeting with Miss Bradshaw on Monday morning. What did the secretary say?

Example: (1) *I'm sorry, Miss Bradshaw's diary is full. She will be talking to Mrs Lewis about the Compact order at eight o'clock.*

2 **Make polite requests using the future progressive with *will* (e.g. *Will you be doing . . .?*) in these situations.**

1 Later today you want to use the computer that your colleague at the office uses.
2 You are sharing a flat with George. You have done the washing up all this week. You want George to do the washing up next week.
3 This evening you need your mother's car to pick your friends up. You are not sure if your mother will need it herself.

3 **Choose verbs from the list to complete the sentences. Use the future perfect (e.g. *will have done . . .*).**

not think, start, dance, not turn off, build, do

1 I hope they ____ everything I gave them to do.
2 We are late. I expect they ____ dinner without us.
3 ____ the Americans ____ that huge space station by the end of this year?
4 By the end of the evening she ____ with every boy in the disco.
5 I suppose the children ____ the central heating. They ____ of it.

4 **Put in the future perfect of the verb in brackets.**

By the next century perhaps we [1]____ (learn) to read each other's minds. Perhaps we also [2]____ (discover) how to move objects through space using our minds only. But some things we are now looking for so hard, we [3]____ (not/find) at all, just as in the Middle Ages we never discovered how to turn metal into gold. And [4]____ (we/contact) other forms of life on other planets? [5]____ (we/learn) to communicate with them? Yes! Definitely! Yes!

25

Infinitive and *-ing* form I: infinitives without an object

A Starting activities

1 What follows?

Verb + infinitive with and without *to* or verb + *-ing*?

1 Work as a class. Some verbs are always followed by the *-ing* form, some are always followed by the infinitive, and some are always followed by the infinitive without *to*. Put the verbs below into three lists: verb + *-ing*, verb + infinitive, verb + infinitive without *to*. To help you decide which list each verb should go in, make sentences like this: *We want to go.*

Verbs: *want, risk, should, promise, avoid, would rather, keep on, offer, refuse, suggest, tend, postpone, deny, ought to*

When you have finished, look at Activity note 29 on page 144.

2 Either as a class or in pairs think of two sentences for each of the verbs below. In one sentence each verb must be followed by *-ing* and in the other sentence it must be followed by the infinitive. What is the difference in meaning?

Verbs: *forget, remember, stop*

I remember locking the door.

I remembered to lock the door.

When you have finished, look at Activity note 34 on page 146.

2 Snap!

Memorizing verbs + infinitive and verbs + *-ing*

1 Work on your own. Make eight 'cards' by folding two pieces of paper in four and tearing along the folds. Write a different sentence on each 'card'. All of the sentences must have a verb from the **Verb 1** list (below) in them (use the past simple tense), followed by a verb from the **Verb 2** list below. Start and finish the sentence in any way that makes sense.
Examples:
We arranged to go to London together.
He put off doing the housework.

Verb 1: *arrange, agree, choose, decide, dislike, finish, enjoy, expect, fancy, give up, hope, keep, keep on, learn, offer, promise, put off, refuse, risk, stop, suggest, want*

Verb 2: *going, to go, smoking, to drive, doing, to help, watching, to get, to lend, asking, to make, getting, losing, lending, to speak, to pay for*

2 Work in pairs. Change cards with your partner and check that the eight sentences that your partner wrote are correct.

3 Work in the same pairs. Change cards with another pair, so that you and your partner both have cards you have not seen before. Play a card and say the sentence on it. Your partner plays one of her or his cards and says the sentence on it. If the *second* verb (from the **Verb 2** list) is the same then call out 'Snap!'. The first person to call takes both cards. The first person with all eight cards is the winner.

B Grammar guide

1 Verb + infinitive

*She promised **to help** me.*

- These verbs are followed by the infinitive:

(can) afford	beg	happen	plan	threaten
agree	not care	hesitate	prepare	volunteer
aim	choose	hope	pretend	(can't) wait
appear	dare	learn	promise	want
arrange	decide	long	refuse	wish
ask	expect	manage	seem	
attempt	fail	offer	tend	

- If there are two infinitives following the verb, joined by *and, but, or, except* or *than,* we don't use *to* before the second infinitive.
  She wanted to sit down and read the paper.

2 Verb + infinitive without *to*

*You can **go** now.*

- All modal verbs are followed by the infinitive without *to*: *can, could, may, might, must, need, ought to, shall, should, will, would.*
- *Would rather, would sooner* and *had better* are also followed by the infinitive without *to.*
  I would rather do it now than later. OR *I'd rather not do it later.*

3 Verb + *-ing* form

*He enjoys **playing** football and **reading** books.*

The most useful verbs that are followed by the *-ing* form are: *admit, advise, avoid, carry on, consider, delay, deny, dislike, enjoy, fancy, finish, give up, imagine, keep, keep on, mention, (not) mind, miss, postpone, practise, put off, recommend, risk, suggest.*

4 Verb + infinitive or *-ing* form

- The most useful verbs that can be followed by the infinitive or by the *-ing* form are: *begin, continue, like, love, hate, intend, prefer, propose, start.*
  Then he began to tell us what had happened. OR *. . . began telling . . .*
- After *would like/love/hate/prefer* we usually use the infinitive.
  I would love to ask you a question.
- These verbs can be followed by the infinitive or by the *-ing* form but there is a change of meaning: *forget, remember, regret, go on, try, stop.*
  With *forget, remember* and *regret* the infinitive is 'before the action' and the *-ing* form is 'after the action'.
  He remembered to lock the door. (remembered before locking)
  He remembered locking the door. (remembered after locking)
  Go on with the infinitive means 'do something different'.
  He started as a clerk and went on to be a film star.
  Go on with the *-ing* form means 'continue'.
  He went on being a film star for ten years.
  Try with the infinitive means 'do your best'.
  She tried to explain on the phone.
  Try with the *-ing* form means 'experiment'.
  Try writing to him, not phoning.
  The infinitive after *stop* gives the reason for stopping.
  Mr Barton stopped to talk to Mrs Drury.
  The *-ing* form after *stop* means the action ended.
  He stopped talking when he saw Mrs Drury wasn't listening.

C Activities

1 Changing places

Verbs + infinitive (with and without *to*), verbs + *-ing*

1 Work on your own. There have been many books and films about two people changing lives with each other. Imagine that you are going to change lives with someone. Imagine that you are going to live in their house, drive their car, do their job. Write sentences about your life so that the person you are going to change with knows everything about you. Give them some advice if you can. Use as many as possible of the verbs below followed by the infinitive, infinitive without *to*, or *-ing* form.
Examples:
I dislike eating lunch, so make sure you can go all day without food.
Prepare to look after a very lively eight-year-old child.
You must avoid feeling overworked. I work at least ten hours a day.
I manage to write a bit as well as teaching.

Verbs

afford	finish	like	remember
avoid	forget	love	seem
begin	go on	manage	start
choose	happen	mean	stop
decide	hate	offer	suggest
dislike	help	prefer	try
enjoy	hope	prepare	want
expect	intend	promise	wish
fail	keep	recommend	would rather
feel like	learn	refuse	would sooner

2 Work in pairs. Imagine that you are going to change lives with your partner. Tell each other about your lives using the sentences you have written. (Correct each other's sentences if necessary.)

3 Work as a class. Tell the class about your partner's life. List the verbs + *-ing*, verbs + infinitive and verbs + infinitive without *to* which other people use in three columns. Who in the class would you most like to change lives with?

2 John considered going to the post office

Verbs + infinitive (with and without *to*), verbs + *-ing*

1 Work in pairs or groups. Tell or write a story which starts *John considered going to the post office.* EVERY sentence of your story must have one of the verbs below in it.

Verbs

admit	enjoy	keep	promise
afford	escape	learn	refuse
agree	expect	let	remember
arrange	fail	manage	risk
ask	fancy	mean	stop
avoid	feel like	mention	seem
beg	finish	(not) mind	start
care	forget	miss	suggest
choose	forgive	offer	try
consider	give up	postpone	want
dare	help	practise	wish
decide	hesitate	put off	would rather
delay	hope	prepare	would sooner
dislike	imagine	pretend	

2 Work as a class. Tell your story to the class.

D Accuracy practice

1 Write the sentences again using the infinitive or *-ing* form.

1 How about going to Scotland for our holiday this year?
We could ______
2 I don't really want to go out this evening.
I'd rather not ______
3 Feed the cat twice a day. Please don't forget.
Please remember ______
4 I definitely paid for these tins at the checkout.
I remember ______
5 It would be dangerous to play tennis before your arm gets better.
Don't risk ______

2 Complete the sentences with the correct form of these verbs:

find, go on, go out, do, come back

1 We'll have to postpone ___ for a drink with Richard. He's ill.
2 Jane has suggested ___ here after the party. What do you think?
3 You can't afford ___ spending money like this, you know.
4 He hoped ___ a cottage to rent in the country.
5 Hey! Nobody mentioned ___ the washing up before we go out.

3 Maria is learning English and working as an au pair in England. This is part of her letter to her elder sister Anna, who teaches English in Italy. Put the verbs in brackets into the infinitive or the *-ing* form.

I want [1]___ (write) to you in English [2]___ (see) if I can do it. Also, my teacher suggested that I try [3]___ (speak) and [4]___ (write) as much English as possible. Well, do you remember all the problems I had at the beginning? My landlady gave me so much work [5]___ (do) that I seemed [6]___ (be) busy all day. As soon as I had finished [7]___ (change) the baby's nappy I had to take the children to school then come home and start [8]___ (make) the beds, [9]___ (do) the washing up and [10]___ (clean) the house. Well, Anna, all that is finished now. Last week the au pair agency offered [11]___ (find) me a new family. And guess what . . .

4 Maria and her new family in England, Mr and Mrs Grant, had a party last week. The neighbours, Mr and Mrs Adams, complained. Here is part of a letter from a solicitor (a lawyer). Put the verbs in brackets into the infinitive or the *-ing* form.

. . . and it seems that Mr and Mrs Grant admitted [1]___ (make) a lot of noise but still refused [2]___ (turn down) the CD player. Mr Adams said that he was prepared [3]___ (accept) the high level of noise until midnight but that he would not hesitate [4]___ (call) the police then if the party continued [5]___ (disturb) the entire street. Mrs Grant laughed and promised [6]___ (invite) Mr Adams to the next party if he would like [7]___ (come). Mr Adams considered [8]___ (say) something rude in reply but decided not to.

26

Adjectives and adverbs that make sentences stronger or weaker

1 Starting off

Making sentences stronger or weaker

1 Work as a class. Look at these examples with *really*, *fairly* and *absolute*.

a *really* (adverb) + verb: *I really hope you can come to the party.*

b *absolute* (adjective) + noun: *John behaved like an absolute idiot.*

c *fairly* (adverb) + adjective: *My parents' car is fairly old now.*

Which of the words (a–c) above make the sentence stronger and which make the sentence weaker?

When you have finished, look at Activity note 25 on page 142.

2 Work in pairs. Now make the three sentences below stronger or weaker by adding one of the words (a–c) to each one.

(i) (stronger) She's a beginner at English.
(ii) (weaker) He's a good guitarist.
(iii) (stronger) I enjoy going to the theatre.

When you have finished, look at Activity note 26 on page 143.

2 She made a complete fool of herself

Making sentences stronger

1 Work in pairs. Make the sentences (i–iii) stronger using the adjectives in brackets. Then explain what happened. (Make this up.) Example:
She made a complete fool of herself at the party. She got excited while she was dancing and broke the CD player.

(i) He made a fool of himself in the lesson. (complete)
(ii) What she told me was nonsense. (absolute)
(iii) Everything we did was a waste of time. (total)

2 Do the same as in 1, using the adverbs in brackets. Example:
I completely agreed with what she said. I was wrong when I argued with her before.

(i) She disagreed and said he should apologize. (totally)
(ii) She is right about Shane's birthday. (absolutely)
(iii) He wasted the opportunity. (completely)

When you have finished, look at Activity note 21 on page 141.

3 Not an interesting day at all

Making sentences weaker

1 Work as a class. Look at these examples with the adverbs *pretty*, *fairly*, and *slightly*.
pretty + adjective: *Anne's office is pretty small.*
fairly + adjective: *The coffee was fairly hot.*
a + *fairly* + adjective: *Sue has a fairly small flat.*
slightly + verb: *Jane's slightly worried about Sarah.*

2 Work in pairs or alone. Write sentences about an ordinary day in the life of an ordinary man. Write about his breakfast, his journey to work, his work at the office, his lunch, what he watched on television in the evening and so on. Each sentence must contain one of the adverbs in 1 (*fairly*, *pretty*, *slightly*). Example: *He had a cup of fairly hot coffee for breakfast.*

3 Work as a class. Read some of your sentences to the class and write down any interesting sentences that other people in the class wrote.

B Grammar guide

1 Adjectives and adverbs

We can use adjectives or adverbs to make sentences stronger or weaker. For example, we can make a sentence like *The party was a success* stronger by using an adjective: *The party was an enormous success.* Some of the adverbs that make sentences stronger or weaker (adverbs of degree) are formed by adding *-ly* to the adjective. (For example, *enormous* becomes *enormously.*)
The party was enormously enjoyable.
Everybody at the party enjoyed it enormously.

2 Making sentences stronger (adverbs)

- The adverbs *absolutely, completely* and *totally* can go in front of verbs to make them stronger.
  I absolutely disagree with you.
- The adverbs *very* and *extremely* can go in front of adverbs or adjectives only.
  We get on very well together. (*well* = adverb)
  She's behaving extremely bravely. (*bravely* = adverb)
  He's a very silly boy. (*silly* = adjective)
  She's extremely healthy. (*healthy* = adjective)
- *Really* makes other adverbs, adjectives, or verbs stronger.
  We get on really well together. (*well* = adverb)
  They've got a really big car. (*big* = adjective)
  Sid really irritates me. (*irritates* = verb)

3 Making sentences stronger (adjectives)

We can also make sentences stronger by putting adjectives in front of nouns. Some of the adjectives we can use to do this are: *absolute, complete, real* and *total.*
I think Jack is an absolute fool. He spends all his money on clothes.
Reading that book was a complete waste of time. It told me nothing new.
This dress was a real bargain. It only cost £10.
The party was a total disaster. Only a few people came and they didn't talk to each other.

4 Making sentences weaker (adverbs)

Four of the most common adverbs which we use to make sentences weaker are *fairly, quite, pretty* and *slightly.*
Fairly, pretty and *slightly* can go before an adverb or an adjecive to make it weaker.
He plays the guitar fairly well. (He is a good, but not a very good, guitar player.)
It was a pretty good film. (I liked it, but I've seen better films.)
Slightly makes the sentence even weaker than *fairly* and *pretty.*
I was slightly surprised to see you. (I was only a little surprised.)
Quite can go before an adverb, adjective or verb to make it weaker.
John paints quite well, but he should try to paint easier subjects. (*well* = adverb)
Tina is quite good at tennis but not very good. (*good* = adjective)
Mr Johnson quite likes his job, but he would like to earn more. (*likes* = verb)
Note that we say *a pretty good film, a fairly good film,* but that we say *quite a good film.*
Tina is quite a good tennis player.

C Activities

1 Wanted by the police

Adjectives and adverbs

1 Work in pairs. Some people in your class are wanted by the police. (Why? As witnesses to a crime?) Write complete descriptions of two or three people in your class and include information on where the police should look for them. Use as many adjectives and adverbs that make sentences stronger or weaker as possible. Examples: *She's a really beautiful woman. He's a very good-looking man.* *You can be fairly sure that she'll be at home in her room in the evenings, studying English grammar.*

2 Present your descriptions to the whole class without saying who you are describing. Can the class guess who the people are? Can they add any more adjectives and adverbs that make sentences stronger or weaker to your descriptions?

2 David and Goliath

Adjectives and adverbs

1 Work in pairs or in three groups. Look at one of the groups of adjectives and adverbs below and put as many as possible into the story of David and Goliath. You can change the story as much as you want to and add new words and sentences if you like. Make sure that you know the vocabulary below before you start.

Vocabulary: shepherd, stone, harp, palace, army, enemy, battle, sword

Group 1: *enormous, completely, extremely, real, fairly*

Group 2: *totally, enormously, really, slightly, quite*

Group 3: *absolutely, very, complete, total, pretty*

David and Goliath

David was a shepherd. He used to sit in the sunshine watching the sheep, throwing stones or playing his harp. People came up the mountain to listen to him playing. David even played for King Saul, at the king's palace. David's music made the king forget, for a while, that the army of his old enemies, the Philistines, was coming from the north. David had three brothers in King Saul's army. One day he went to take them some food. King Saul's army was facing the Philistines, waiting for the battle. Then a huge man, a Philistine, stepped forward. His name was Goliath. He asked for someone from King Saul's army to come out and fight him. David said that he wanted to fight Goliath. Little David walked towards the Philistine army wearing only his long shirt and carrying his shepherd's stick. As he walked he picked up a stone. Goliath and the Philistine army laughed at him. David threw the stone at Goliath. It hit him on the head and he fell. David ran forward, took Goliath's own sword and killed him. The Philistine army turned and ran. King Saul's army had won.

2 Work as a class. Read your version of the story to the whole class. Listen to other people's versions of the story. Could any more words or different words from the groups in 1 be put in?

D Accuracy practice

1 Complete the sentences using the words below.

complete (×3), *completely* (×2), *extremely* (×5)

1 All the computers were ____ destroyed in the fire.
2 I am ____ sorry to hear the bad news about your father's illness.
3 It was a ____ surprise when he found out that Valerie was in London.
4 You are an ____ silly young man.
5 The party was a ____ disaster.
6 The sports facilities in the area are ____ good.
7 It was a ____ waste of time going to see such an ____ boring film.
8 Joanne always gets on ____ well with Jack although she ____ disagrees with his political opinions.

2 Complete the sentences using one of the words in brackets.

1 Goliath was an ____ man. (enormous, enormously)
2 This is his first piano lesson. He's an ____ beginner. (absolute, absolutely)
3 Julie plays the guitar ____ well. (extreme, extremely)
4 I ____ like talking to you. (very, really, extremely)
5 Rebecca speaks Italian ____ fluently, but she makes a lot of mistakes with the grammar. (real, quite, total)
6 Didn't you like the film? I ____ enjoyed it. (fairly, quite, pretty)
7 Robin paints ____ marvellously. (total, really, absolute)
8 We got on ____ well, as soon as we met. (completely, slightly, extremely)
9 There was ____ no need to tell Jane such bad news at this time. (absolutely, absolute, very)
10 I think reading this book was a ____ waste of time. (pretty, totally, total)
11 He plays football ____ well, but he's not good enough for the club team. (totally, fairly, absolutely)
12 Young Tom is ____ clever at working out difficult problems. (real, absolutely, quite)

3 Put in the missing words from the list below.

real, enormous, slightly, absolutely, extremely

'It is important that you are [1]____ clear about this,' said the woman in charge of the rescue work. 'We have an [2]____ dangerous situation here. There has been an [3]____ landslide and some of the houses have slipped down the hill. The situation has improved [4]____ since it stopped raining, but it is still dangerous as there is a [5]____ danger of starting another landslide.

27

Prepositions after verbs, adjectives and nouns

A Starting activities

1 Preposition grids

Prepositions after verbs, adjectives and nouns

1 Work in pairs or small groups. Copy out *one* of the grids below. Tick (✓) if a combination is possible and cross (×) if it is not possible.

Grid 1	of	for	with	about	at	on
laugh	×	×	×	✓		
decide						
ask						
negotiate						
dream						
worry						

Grid 2	at	with	by	of	for	to	about
fed up	×	✓					
surprised							
married							
nice							
amused							
bored							

Grid 3	for	in	of	to	with
sympathy	✓	×	×		
photograph					
reaction					
exception					
damage					
recipe					

When you have finished, look at Activity note 38 on page 147.

2 Work in the same pairs or small groups. Decide whether the grid you chose contains verbs, adjectives or nouns. Think of at least three more verbs, adjectives or nouns which can be used with the prepositions in your grid. You can use the lists in the Grammar guide or use other verbs, adjectives or nouns. Make at least three sentences using the three new words you have added and prepositions from the grid. Read your sentences to the class.
Example: *My friends were very* ***rude to*** *the waiter at the restaurant so the next day I went back there and* ***apologized for*** *their behaviour.*

2 I'll pay for the holiday

Prepositions after verbs, adjectives and nouns

1 Work in pairs. Take it in turns to persuade your partner *either* to go on holiday with you, *or* to share a flat with you, *or* to marry you. In each case your partner does not want to. (Why not?) Use as many prepositions after verbs, adjectives and nouns as you can, from the lists in the Grammar guide or others. Remember the combinations you use and count them after you have finished talking.
Example: *I have a* ***photograph of*** *the flat here.*

2 Work as a class. Who used the highest number of combinations of prepositions after verbs, nouns and adjectives? Tell the class which combinations you used and how you used them. List any interesting combinations that are not listed in the Grammar guide.

B Grammar guide

Particular prepositions combine with particular verbs, adjectives or nouns. Here are some of the most important combinations. If you are not sure of any meanings, look them up in a good dictionary such as the *Oxford Advanced Learner's Dictionary.*

1 Verbs + prepositions

*Jenny **paid for** the meal.*

doing
borrow something from*
deal with
introduce someone to*
laugh about something
laugh at someone
lend something to*
pay for
wait for

speaking
apologize to/for
argue about
ask someone about/for*
complain about
confess to
explain something to
negotiate with
talk about/to
thank someone for*

feeling
ashamed of
believe in
dream about
hope for
worry about

Note that verbs + prepositions marked * are used in verb + *someone/something* + preposition constructions. *Sue introduced her new boyfriend to her family.*

2 Adjectives + prepositions

*John was **excited about** the party.*

*I am **used to** working on my own.*

positive
amused at/by/about
excited about
good at
interested in
kind of/to
interested in
nice to/of/about
pleased with
proud of

negative
ashamed of
bad at
bored with/by
critical of
disappointed in
fed up with/about
suspicious of
upset about
worried about

descriptive
different from
full of
engaged to
identical to
married to
responsible for
similar to
sure about
used to

fear
afraid of
anxious about
frightened of
scared of
terrified of

surprise and anger
amazed at/by
angry at/with
annoyed at
shocked at/by/about
surprised at/by

3 Nouns + prepositions

*Ann gave me a **cheque for** £30.00.*

abstract
advantage of
addiction to
connection with/between
damage to
disadvantage of
exception to/of
increase in
reaction to
sympathy for

concrete
cheque for
friend of
invitation to
photograph of
recipe for
reply to
witness to

C Activities

1 How to write a short play

Prepositions after verbs, adjectives and nouns

1 Work in pairs, A and B. Together, choose five adjective, noun or verb + preposition combinations. Use the lists in the Grammar guide to give you ideas, but use others if you want to. You are going to write a dialogue based on one of the situations below. Choose (a), (b) or (c).

Situations

a A is the host of a party, B is a gatecrasher.
b A is someone whose flat has just been burgled and B is a friend who is advising her/him.
c A is someone who needs money badly (what for?) and B is a friend who is giving advice.

2 Work in pairs, sitting opposite each other. Decide who is A and who is B. You need one piece of paper between the two of you. A starts the dialogue by writing who he or she is, and writing the first thing he or she wants to say. A then passes the piece of paper to B who reads what A wrote and writes a reply, like this:
A writes:
HOST *What are you doing here?*
(A passes the paper to B.)
B writes:
GATECRASHER *Er, I'm a friend of John's.*
(B passes the paper to A.)

A and B must not talk to each other and must not co-operate in any way. The dialogue must include the five adjective, noun or verb + preposition combinations that you chose. They must come up naturally in the dialogue without any advance planning by A and B.

3 Work as a class. With your partner, read your dialogue aloud to the class.

2 The memory game

Prepositions after adjectives, nouns and verbs

1 Work in pairs or small groups. First, set up the game. Take four pieces of paper per pair or group and fold each piece of paper in half three times. Tear along the creases to make thirty-two small squares of paper per pair or group. On one side of each piece of paper write an adjective + preposition, noun + preposition or verb + preposition. Use the list in the Grammar guide to give you ideas but use others if you want to. Turn the pieces of paper face down so that you cannot see the adjectives, nouns and verbs + prepositions.

2 Work in pairs or small groups. Play the game as follows. Each player takes it in turn to turn over two pieces of paper and read aloud what is on them. If the two pieces of paper have the same preposition the player keeps them, if not the player turns them back face down, keeping them in the same place. You must try to remember where certain prepositions are. The player who has the most pieces of paper at the end of the game is the winner.

3 Trouble at Hamlet's castle: almost everybody is dead

Prepositions after adjectives, nouns and verbs

Work in pairs or groups or as a class. Imagine that any story from history or fiction has just happened and write it as a newspaper report in one or two paragraphs. Include as many adjective, noun and verb + preposition combinations as you naturally can. Here are some ideas for stories from elsewhere in the book, but use your own ideas if you want to: *Hamlet* (Unit 20, page 86), *King Lear* (Unit 29, page 122), *Cinderella* (Activity note 7, page 138).

D Accuracy practice

1 Put in the correct prepositions to complete the sentences.

1 I've been waiting ____ this bus for half an hour now.
2 Three years after she killed her husband, Mrs Sedgely confessed ____ the murder.
3 Don't worry ____ the exams, just do the best you can.
4 We were at the wrong bus stop and so we missed the last bus. We can laugh ____ it now, but it wasn't so funny at the time.
5 I was just talking ____ Sarah when she walked in!
6 Helen's dress is two sizes too big. She borrowed it ____ her sister.
7 My cat has run away before but never so far. I really want to thank you ____ bringing him back.
8 Mrs Ridgeway, I really must apologize ____ my brother. I thought he was very rude to you last night.

2 Put in the correct prepositions after the adjectives to complete the sentences.

1 He was very upset ____ what had happened.
2 I have always been suspicious ____ people who don't tell you anything about themselves.
3 I'm bored ____ watching television every evening.
4 We were all amazed ____ how much she knew about Britain.
5 You did very well. I'm proud ____ you.

3 Put in the correct prepositions after the nouns to complete the sentences.

1 One advantage ____ this motorbike is that it is very reliable.
2 Addiction ____ drugs is one of the worst things that can happen to anyone.
3 What's the connection ____ this book and your holiday in Switzerland?
4 Harry saw the police talking to Jennifer. She was a witness ____ a bad road accident.
5 It really wasn't Sean's fault. I've got a lot of sympathy ____ him.

4 Prepositions after verbs, adjectives and nouns in context. Two colleagues are discussing someone they work with. Put in the missing prepositions.

MS LONG Is Mr Smedley responsible [1]____ all customer complaints? It's just that there's been a big increase [2]____ complaints lately and some of them aren't dealt [3]____ for months.

MR McLAREN I know. I don't like to be critical [4]____ a colleague, but that's the disadvantage [5]____ having someone who is not good [6]____ administration doing a job like this. And he's been doing it for two years now. I mean, he should be used [7]____ answering letters and sending people's money back. But look, there's a cheque [8]____ fifty pounds here. It's been on his desk for five days, and where . . . Ah! Hello, Mr Smedley. I didn't see you standing there. I was, er, just going.

Infinitive and *-ing* form II: infinitives with an object

A Starting activities

1 We advised the Prime Minister to reduce taxes

Verb + object + infinitive

1 Work in pairs. Write down the names of five people. They can be famous people, or friends that you both know, or people in the class. Write five sentences using some of the verbs below with the people on your list as objects. Use the past simple tense. Example: *We advised the Prime Minister to reduce taxes.*

Each pair in the class should work with different verbs from the list so that all the verbs are used.
Verbs: *advise, allow, ask, encourage, expect, force, get, hate, help, invite, mean, need, order, permit, persuade, prefer, recommend, remind, teach, tell, want, warn, wish*

2 Work as a class. One person from each pair reads some of their sentences to the class. Write down any sentences that other people read out which include verbs that you haven't used.

2 Mini dialogues

Verb + question word + infinitive

1 Work in pairs or groups. Choose three sentences from the list of sentences. Make a mini dialogue by writing a sentence before and a sentence after each one. You can change or add words if you need to. Pairs should work with different sentences so that all the sentences are used. Example:
A: *Were all the jackets nice?*
B: *Yes, I didn't know which to choose.*
A: *So which one did you buy in the end?*

List of sentences
I didn't know which to choose.
I haven't decided whether to go or not.
Has she found out what to do?
I was wondering how to tell him.
Ask her who to invite.
Show us where to go, please.

2 Read your mini dialogues to the class.

3 Circus acts

Verb + object + infinitive without *to* OR + *-ing*

Work in pairs. Imagine you are outside a circus, trying to persuade people to come in. Write or say (or shout) sentences about the circus acts with verb + object + infinitive without *to* or + *-ing*. Use *hear, see* and *watch*, like this:
Come and see the fire eater perform.
You will see the fire burning.
Use the pictures below to give you ideas for the circus acts.

B Grammar guide

1 Verb + object + infinitive

They didn't want ***me to go.***

John begged ***her not to leave.***

- These verbs can be followed by an object and an infinitive:

advise	encourage	hate	(would) like	permit	teach
allow	expect	help	mean (= intend)	persuade	tell
ask	force	intend	need	recommend	want
beg	get (= persuade)	invite	order	remind	warn

- We can also use verb + object + infinitive to express purpose (the reason for something), answering the question 'What for?'.
  I can't reach. I need a chair to stand on.

2 Verb + question word + infinitive

I didn't know ***which to choose.***

He remembered ***what to do.***

- These verbs can be followed by a question word (e.g. *which, what, how*) or phrase (e.g. *how many*) and an infinitive: *ask, decide, discover, discuss, explain, find out, forget, know, learn, remember, see, show, tell, understand, wonder.*
- *What, which, whose, how many* and *how much* can be followed by a noun + infinitive.
  We didn't know how many plates to buy.
  NOTE You cannot use this sentence pattern with the question word *why* but you can use *why* like this: *I don't know why I chose that one.*

3 Adjective + infinitive and noun + infinitive

We can use the infinitive after some adjectives (e.g. *pleased, angry, sad, upset*) and after *it* + *be* + adjective.
I'm pleased to meet you. *It is good to be here.*
We can also use the infinitive after some nouns (e.g. *work, job,* and other things that we have to do).
I've got some work to do. *I've got an essay to write by tomorrow.*

4 Verb + object + infinitive without *to*

- The verbs *let* and *make* can be followed by an object + the infinitive without *to.*
  Let him have some sweets after dinner.
  Make him go to bed at nine, or he'll be tired tomorrow.
- Some verbs can be followed by an object and an infinitive without *to* OR by an *-ing* form.
  I saw him switch on the light. OR *I saw him switching on the light.*
  Some useful verbs with this sentence pattern are: *feel, hear, listen to, look at, notice, see, watch.*
  For longer actions, the infinitive is used when the action is complete and the *-ing* form is used when the action is still in progress.
  I heard him come home. (action complete)
  I heard him coming home. (action in progress)

5 Preposition + *-ing* form

Prepositions (e.g. *to, by, of, for*) are followed by the *-ing* form, not by an infinitive.
I look forward ***to*** *seeing you next week.*
Jim avoided the crowds ***by*** *going the long way round.*
Before *becoming a dentist he worked for a computer firm.*

C Activities

1 Mini sagas

Adjective + infinitive, noun + infinitive, preposition + *-ing* form

1 Work in pairs or groups. A mini saga is a story that is exactly fifty words long, not counting the title. Write a mini saga which includes one of these pairs of sentences.

a There is a lot of work to do.
I have a package to deliver tonight.

b It was kind of Joanna to warn me.
She was upset to hear the news.

c After running to the bus-stop she was exhausted.
By telling him that she probably saved his life.

2 Look at the mini sagas written by other pairs or groups in the class. Change them to add more adjective + infinitive, noun + infinitive and preposition + infinitive sentences. Are there any mistakes in the mini sagas?

2 Dialogue pairs

Verb + infinitive or *-ing* form

1 Work in pairs or groups. Put the verbs in the lists below into pairs and make a dialogue (a sentence and a reply) from each pair. Your two sentences must each have an infinitive (with object), or an *-ing* form.
Example (a dialogue with *ask* and *tell*):
A: *Did he ask you to go to the disco with him?*
B: *Yes. But I told him to go with his girlfriend.*

Verb + object + infinitive: *advise, allow, ask, help, invite, persuade, prefer, recommend, tell, want*
Verb + *-ing* form: *dislike, give up, keep, like, put off* (= delay), *stop, suggest*

2 Either form new pairs or join pairs to make groups of four. Use as many of your dialogue pairs as you can to make a continuous dialogue. You can change a dialogue pair in any way you wish, but you must not separate the two sentences of the dialogue pair.

3 Read or act out your dialogue to the rest of the class. Write down any new sentences with infinitive or *-ing* that you hear.

3 Playing games

***-ing* form and infinitive**

1 Work on your own. Make eight 'cards' by folding two pieces of paper in half and then in half again and tearing along the folds. On each 'card' write one of the categories from the list below.

Categories
1 verb + *-ing*
2 verb + infinitive
3 verb + *-ing* or infinitive
4 verb + object + infinitive
5 noun + infinitive
6 adjective + infinitive
7 preposition + *-ing*

2 Work in pairs or groups. One person plays one of his or her eight 'cards' and someone else says a sentence using the category on that 'card'.
Example: verb + *-ing*
John dislikes doing his homework.
You get one point for a correct sentence and the winner is the one with the most points. If you are not sure whether a sentence is correct or not, write it down.

3 Work as a class. Now read out any sentences which you are not sure are correct. Can you say if other people's sentences are correct or not? Write down any correct sentences that are new to you.

D Accuracy practice

1 Put in the infinitive or the *-ing* form of the verb in brackets.

1. I was very happy ____ (see) you there.
2. Jenny succeeds by ____ (work) harder than anybody else.
3. The Tomlinson family were glad ____ (be) back in Australia.
4. The tourists were frightened of ____ (lose) their way in London.
5. She was sad ____ (see) such disappointing exam results.
6. I want someone ____ (share) a flat with me.

2 Write sentences.

1. Henry's girlfriend/persuade/him/see a doctor yesterday.
2. Richard's friends/make/him see that horror film, even though he didn't want to.
3. Juliette's parents/not let/her/stay up later than ten o'clock when she was twelve.
4. I/listen to/the birds/sing when you came in this morning.
5. I/see/Mr Wilson/paint/his house last week. That was before his accident/force/him/leave it half-painted.

3 Guy and his wife Cheryl have known Gillian since they were at school together. Here is part of a letter from Cheryl to Gillian. Put in the infinitive or the *-ing* form of the verbs in brackets.

Guy asked me [1]____ (write) to you ages ago but I've been too busy. You know I was thinking of [2]____ (leave) my job? Well, just when I was finally going to leave, the company offered to send me on a Management Course, so I decided to stay after all. But Guy warned me [3]____ (not/accept) a place on the course unless they had a management job [4]____ (offer) me at the end of it. So I said to Mr Cowans (the boss), 'Don't expect me [5]____ (go on) this course unless . . .'

4 Here is the letter giving Cheryl information about the Management Course. Put in the infinitive or the *-ing* form of the verbs in brackets.

I am pleased [1]____ (confirm) the offer of a place on the 'Management for the Future' course from April 10–14.

Mr Cowans has explained the course to you but may I remind you [2]____ (bring) your four recommendations for [3]____ (improve) your department with you. We will explain how [4]____ (use) your recommendations during the course.

Soap is provided at the Course Centre but we need you [5]____ (bring) your own towels. We ask all course participants not to delay handing in their room keys at the end of the course. After [6]____ (register) with the Course Supervisor at 5.30 p.m. on April 10 we would like you [7]____ (meet) the other participants in room 3B.

29

Indirect (reported) speech

A Starting activities

1 Choices

The tenses in indirect speech

Work as a class. Which of the indirect speech sentences below are correct? If you think both (a) and (b) are correct, try to say what the speaker wants to emphasize in sentence (b).

1 'I love you, Karen.'
   a Roger told Karen that he loved her.
   b Roger told Karen that he loves her.

2 'Is it raining?'
   a Kate asked if it was raining.
   b Kate asked if it is raining.

3 'You've broken my CD player!'
   a Paul told Ann that she had broken his CD player.
   b Paul told Ann that she's broken his CD player.

When you have finished, look at Activity note 58 on page 155.

2 He said, she said

Verbs that introduce indirect speech

Work in pairs. Here are some of the verbs that introduce indirect speech: *say, warn, think, suggest, reply, advise.* Take it in turns to read out the direct speech sentences below. Your partner then says each sentence as indirect speech using one of the possible indirect speech verbs, in the past simple tense. There may be more than one possible answer. Example:

'You have passed the examination.'
She ____ me I have passed the examination.
A: *You have passed the examination.*
B: *She* ***told*** *me I have passed the examination.*

1 'Nice day, isn't it?'
   She ____ it was a nice day.
2 'I think Sheila's coming, but I'm not sure.'
   He ____ Sheila was coming, but he wasn't sure.
3 'Let's go on to a nightclub afterwards.'
   She ____ that we went on to a nightclub afterwards.
4 'Look out!'
   She ____ me to look out.
5 'If I were you I'd spend the money now.'
   Richard ____ me to spend the money now.
6 Tom: 'Are you coming?' Gill: 'Not yet.'
   Gill ____ that she wasn't coming yet.

When you have finished, look at Activity note 23 on page 142.

3 Evelyn and Les

Indirect speech in context

Work in pairs, A and B. With your partner, read the short dialogue between Evelyn and Les. Then put the dialogue into indirect speech starting *Evelyn told Les that . . . and then Les replied . . .* You have your own part of the dialogue only.

Person A: You are Evelyn. Read Activity note 22 on page 142.
Person B: You are Les. Read Activity note 59 on page 155.

B Grammar guide

1 Indirect speech: past

- After a past tense indirect speech verb (like *said* or *told* or *thought*) you can use the same tense as in the direct speech sentence or you can change it.
  DIRECT SPEECH *'I like apples.'* (present simple)
  INDIRECT SPEECH *She said she likes apples.* (present simple) OR *She said she liked apples.* (past simple)
  But change the tense when the information is out of date or not true now. (For example, if she doesn't like apples any more use *liked*.)
- Here are the possible tense changes:

DIRECT SPEECH	INDIRECT SPEECH
'I like apples.'	*She said she liked apples.*
'I'm writing a letter.'	*She said she was writing a letter.*
'I saw the film.'	*She said she had seen the film.*
'I have finished.'	*She said she had finished.*
'I was having lunch.'	*She said she had been having lunch.*
'I will be thirty next month.'	*She said she would be thirty next month.*

- Do not change *would*, *could*, *should* and *ought to* in indirect speech.

2 Indirect speech: present, future and present perfect

After present, future or present perfect indirect speech verbs there is usually no change of tense.
Ron (on the phone to Alan): *'Do you and Jennifer want to go with me?'*
Alan: *'Jennifer, Ron is on the phone. He's asking if we want to go with him.'*

3 Questions in indirect speech

Use *if* or *whether* when you are reporting a question which has no question word.
DIRECT SPEECH *'Is he coming this evening?'*
INDIRECT SPEECH *She asked if* (OR *whether*) *he is* (OR *was*) *coming this evening.*
We can also use *ask* + object + *if/whether* to report a question. *She asked Bill if he was coming.*

4 Imperative in indirect speech

Use *tell* + object + *to* when you are reporting a command or instruction.
DIRECT SPEECH *'Go to the bank tomorrow.'*
INDIRECT SPEECH *He told us to go the bank tomorrow.*

5 Indirect speech verbs with and without *to* or *that*

The verb *ask*, when used to report a request, is followed by an object and *to*.
Trevor asked me to get a newspaper for him.
The verbs *warn*, *remind* and *tell* can be followed by an object and *to* or by an object and *that*.
She told Sarah to be careful. *She told Sarah that she must be careful.*
The verbs *complain*, *exclaim*, *explain*, *think*, *hope*, *say* and *suggest* can be followed by *that* but not by an object.
She said that the rent must be paid. (NOT ~~*She said me*~~)
He suggested that we stayed and watched television. (NOT ~~*He suggested me*~~)
You can leave out the word *that* after *say*, *tell* and *suggest*.
She told Sarah she must be careful.

C Activities

1 Short stories

Direct and indirect speech

1 Work alone. Write the story of any play, film, television programme or novel that you know in less than one hundred words. If you cannot think of a story of your own, use the story of King Lear below.

2 Work in pairs. Put direct speech and indirect speech sentences into your story and your partner's story, using as many of these verbs as you can and other verbs: *think, hope, say, tell, explain, reply, warn.*
Example: *King Lear said that he had decided to divide his kingdom between his daughters.*

> There was an old king (King Lear) who had three daughters. He decided to divide his kingdom between his daughters and give up his power. His advisers and the people who loved him were shocked and worried. The old king went to stay with his two eldest daughters, Goneril and Regan, but they grew tired of him and asked him to leave. The youngest daughter, Cordelia, had left England to marry the King of France. So Lear was left homeless, out in the open air, wandering through fields in a storm. When Cordelia died, Lear died of a broken heart.

3 Work as a class. Read your new version of the story to the class.

2 Great moments from history

Direct and indirect speech

1 Work as a class. Here are some important moments in British history:
William the Conqueror from Normandy defeats King Harold at the Battle of Hastings (1066)
Newton discovers gravity (1687)
England win the football World Cup (1966)

Write down some great moments from your country's history.

2 Work in pairs or small groups. Imagine what the people involved in each great moment of history said at the time, and how it was reported later. Write direct speech and indirect speech sentences, which can be serious or humorous. (By the way, Newton discovered gravity when an apple fell on his head.)
Example:
Newton: *'Ouch! An apple has fallen on my head. This must be gravity.'*
Newton exclaimed that the apple had fallen on his head because of gravity.

3 Work as a class. Read your direct and indirect speech sentences out to the class.

3 Drugs kill

Direct and indirect speech, positive and negative

1 Work in pairs or groups of four. Read the dialogue in Activity note 24 on page 142. If you are working in a group of four you can read it aloud, playing the parts.

2 Work in the same pairs or groups of four. Two years later the Roper family all remembered what everybody said. But, as in life, they all remembered it differently. Read Activity note 67 on page 159. Discuss how the four of them remembered what was said. Who is nearest the truth? And who, in the family, was right and who was wrong? Make indirect speech sentences with both positive and negative indirect speech verbs.
Examples: *Mrs Roper thought that Sheena was taking drugs. Mr Roper did not say that he wanted Sheena to leave home.*

D Accuracy practice

1 Put the direct speech into indirect speech. More than one answer is possible.

1 'I went to a concert with Mary.'
Trevor said ____________

2 'I didn't do any housework.'
Dad explained ____________

3 'Harry doesn't want to dance.'
Tracy said ____________

4 'I am paying for the bread.'
He told us ____________

5 'I've finished!'
She said ____________

2 Put the direct speech questions into indirect speech. Use *asked* + object + *if*. Change the tense of the verb in the direct speech.

1 Mr Williams: 'John, did you find the hammer?'
Mr Williams asked John if he ____________

2 Ms Fowler: 'Dave, are you from Edinburgh?'

3 Jenny: 'Jean, do you know what "versatile" means?'

4 Lynn: 'Will you go out with David again, Tessa?'

5 Peter: 'Susan, are you playing tennis on Friday?'

3 Write indirect speech sentences. Put the indirect speech verb (*tell* and *ask*) into the past simple, and use *to* (e.g. *she told him to*).

1 She/tell/Peter/remember/his keys.

2 The Managing Director/tell/everybody/expect/a good profit.

3 The teacher/tell/Kate/do/some extra homework.

4 Henry/ask/Gemma/marry/him/three times last year.

4 Use the verbs in brackets to make indirect speech sentences. Change the tense of the verb in direct speech where you can.

1 (explained) Brian: 'You should press the red button, Henry.'
Brian explained that Henry ____________

2 (told) Mary: 'You look pale, Lesley. You should see a doctor.'
Mary told Lesley to ____________

3 (thought) Tim: 'More people ought to use recycled paper.'
Tim thought that ____________

4 (hoped) James: 'It will snow this winter.'
James ____________

5 (suggested) Richard: 'Why don't we go out for a meal?'
Richard ____________

6 (said) Gemma: 'I've had a good day at work.'
Gemma ____________

30

The position and order of adverbs

A Starting activities

1 Matching them up

Learning the rules by finding examples

1 Work as a class. Here are some rules about adverb position and order and some examples of the rules. Match the rules with the examples.

Rules

a Adverbs of manner usually come after the verb.
b Sentence adverbs are often the first word in the sentence.
c Adverbs of place and adverb phrases usually come after the verb.
d Adverbs of frequency usually come before the main verb.

Examples

(i) *Unfortunately*, Rosie did not get to the station in time.
(ii) When I was a boy, I would *often* sit and listen to my parents talking until late at night.
(iii) A large white mouse sat *under the table.*
(iv) James Bond looked *carefully* round the room.

When you have finished, look at Activity note 65 on page 158.

2 Work as a class. Decide if the adverbs below are sentence adverbs, or adverbs of manner, or place, or frequency.

Adverbs: *beautifully, here, always, actually, angrily, frequently*

2 Ron from Mars

Adverbs of frequency, manner and place

Work as a class or in pairs. Ron has just arrived from the planet Mars. Describe as many of the following as you can to Ron: a cat, a computer, a disco, a tennis match. Remember Ron has not seen any of them before. Include as many adverbs of frequency, manner and place as you realistically can. Example: *A cat frequently sits in the sun washing itself energetically.*

B Grammar guide

1	**Adverbs of manner** (like *beautifully, secretly, carefully*)	Adverbs of manner (e.g. *beautifully*) usually come after the verb. *Caroline sings beautifully.* But they can also come after the object (e.g. *that song*) if there is one. *Caroline sings that song beautifully.* If the object is long (e.g. *not to tell him*) they can sometimes come before the verb. *They secretly decided not to tell him.*
2	**Adverbs of place** (like *here, there, north, away, abroad*)	Adverbs of place usually come after the verb. *Did you drive here?* *He looked everywhere for the money.* But they can also come after the object. *He looked for the money everywhere.* Adverb phrases with a preposition as the first word are used in the same way. *The cat is sitting under the table.* (adverb phrase after the verb) *He looked for the money in all the wrong places.* (adverb phrase after the object)
3	**Adverbs of time** (like *afterwards, lately, soon, yesterday, since Tuesday, on Sunday*)	Adverbs of time usually come at the beginning or the end of a sentence. *I saw her yesterday.* *Tomorrow we are going to London.* But *yet* can come before the verb. *We have not yet started discussing the details.* Adverb phrases of time can start with *since, for, at once, until* and *then.* *We waited until the shops closed.*
4	**Adverbs of frequency** (like *ever, never, often, always*)	Adverbs of frequency usually come before the main verb but they come after *to be.* *I sometimes go with him.* *He is always late.* If there is an auxiliary verb they come after the first auxiliary. *I have often told you about her.* *Sometimes, occasionally* and *frequently* can also come at the beginning of the sentence. *Sometimes I feel so sad.*
5	**Adverbs of degree** (like *fairly, hardly, just, quite, very, extremely*)	Adverbs of degree usually come before the adjective or adverb they modify. *The party didn't finish until fairly late.* If the adverb of degree modifies a verb it comes before the main verb. *She is just leaving.* *They had hardly started the race, when it began to rain.* *Really* can come early in the sentence for more emphasis. *You really should stop smoking.*
6	**Sentence adverbs** (like *actually, anyway, of course*)	We use sentence adverbs to say what we feel about a whole sentence. These adverbs are usually the first word in the sentence. *Unfortunately, Rosie did not get to the station in time.*
7	**The order of adverbs**	When we have a number of adverbs in a sentence, the most usual order is manner, then place, then time. *They worked hard in the garden today.* NOTE There are many exceptions to the rules about the position and order of adverbs.

C Activities

1 A three-day search for hidden treasure

Position of adverbs

1 Work as a class. Suggest three valuable items of 'treasure'. (Examples: *an expensive computer, one thousand pounds in cash.*) Then suggest at least three places in your school or in the area around the place where you are learning English where each item could be hidden. Example: *The computer could be hidden behind the dustbins in the car park.* Each suggestion must use an adverb phrase of place. Your teacher will listen to your suggestions and decide where the three items are hidden, but won't tell you yet.

2 Work in pairs or groups. Imagine and describe a three-day search for the three items of treasure. Include as many adverbs as you naturally can. Use the list of verbs below to help you. Include two surprising incidents or problems that you had when you were looking for the hidden treasure. Example: *On the first day, we were looking carefully through the cupboards in the classroom when one of the teachers came in and rudely asked us to leave the building.*
Say where you found each item of treasure.

Verbs: *look for, search, go through, think of (looking), come up with (an idea), dig, dig up*

3 Work as a class. Tell the rest of the class about your three-day search and make a note of the adverbs that other groups or pairs use when they describe their search. Your teacher will then tell you where the treasure was actually hidden.

2 Adverb game

Position of adverbs

1 Work in pairs, A and B. You need one piece of paper between the two of you.

- **Person A:** Write the first part of a sentence putting in someone's name (the name of someone famous, or the name of someone in the class perhaps), a verb and an adverb of manner.

> (Name) was (verb) (adverb of manner) along the street when he/she . . .

Fold the paper so B cannot see what you wrote and pass it to B.

- **Person B:** Write this part of a sentence putting in someone's name, an adverb of manner and an adverb phrase of place.

> saw (name) going (adverb of manner) into a shop (adverb phrase of place).

Fold the paper so A cannot see what you wrote and pass it to A.

- **Person A:** Write this sentence putting in an adverb of frequency.

> 'Do you (adverb of frequency) go in there?'

Fold the paper and pass it to B.

- **Person B:** Write this sentence putting in a sentence adverb, an adverb of frequency and a noun.

> '(Sentence adverb) I (adverb of frequency) go in there to buy my (noun).'

2 Open the paper out and change the story, if you need to, until it makes sense.

3 Read the story out to the class.

D Accuracy practice

1 Where can we put the adverb in brackets in these sentences? More than one answer is sometimes possible.

1 I go to the cinema on my own. (sometimes)
2 We had finished eating when the door bell rang. (hardly)
3 She ought not to argue all the time. (really)
4 Do you want to change your job? (ever)
5 I will know how he managed to do it. (never)
6 She takes an afternoon off work. (often)
7 She is one of the last to leave. (often)

2 Is the adverb or adverb phrase printed in *italics* in the correct place? If it is not, move it to a correct place.

1 *Always* I forget to give you my homework.
2 He has not *yet* answered my letter.
3 Richard has *since four o'clock* been on the phone.
4 He is *extremely* good at dealing with problems quickly.
5 Jerry *quite* dances well actually.
6 You must listen to me when I'm talking to you *really*.
7 He has *lately* been very depressed.
8 I will *on Thursday* give you any necessary information.
9 We can't *anyway* go yet, it's too early.
10 She isn't ready to play *of course* for the club team.

3 Write these sentences with the phrase or phrases in brackets in the right order, and in a correct place in the sentence.

1 There's a brown file. (the/in/desk/drawer)
2 I'll see you. (on/here/Monday)
3 She always criticizes your work. (a/way/in/very/polite)
4 I ordered a new computer. (ago/a/weeks/few)
5 Please put that down. (over/carefully/before/you/there/go)

4 Complete the story using the adverbs below. Use each word once.

far, unhappily, back, everywhere, there, cheerfully, around, never, often

There is a homeless old man living near here who I [1]____ see in the mornings wandering [2]____ the field near my house. He [3]____ goes very [4]____ from the field. He sleeps [5]____ too, in a large box under a tree. One day I lost some papers. 'I'll just have to do all that work again', I said [6]____. Then I thought the papers might have fallen out of my case on the way to my house. So I searched [7]____ in the field but I could not see the papers. I was just on my way [8]____ home when the old man appeared with the papers. He grinned [9]____. 'There are three mistakes in this report', he said. 'How do you know?' I said. 'I know a lot about your company', he said, 'I used to be the Managing Director.'

31

Link words

A Starting activities

1 Packing for the holiday

and and _but_ type link words

1 Work as a class. Decide on one place where you all want to go for a two week holiday.

2 Work alone. Write down everything you want to take with you on holiday. Include clothes, things like a hairdryer, books, games, anything you think you might need.

3 Work in pairs. You can take only one suitcase each on holiday. Each of you can take only half of what you decided you wanted to take. Discuss what you and your partner should take and what you should leave behind. Use these *and* and *but* type of link words as often as you realistically can: *also, and, neither . . . nor, but, either . . . or.*
Examples: *You can take either your blue dress or the brown one.*
I want to take my hairdryer but I also need some towels.

2 It was snowing, so we stayed indoors

Cause and result link words

1 Work in pairs, A and B. A writes three sentences about what the weather has been like in the last few days. B writes three clauses that are the result of hot, cold, windy, wet or dry weather. B's clauses must begin with *so*. Do not look at what the other person is writing.
Example:
A: *It was very hot yesterday.*
B: *so we wore raincoats and took umbrellas.*

2 Work in the same pairs. Look at what you both wrote and create three sentences that make sense, changing some words if necessary, for example, change *hot* to *wet.* Example:
It was very wet yesterday so we wore raincoats and took umbrellas.

3 Work in the same pairs. Do the same as in 1 and 2, but this time B writes three sentences about what she or he did last weekend and A writes three clauses beginning with *because* or *because of* about why she or he (A) did something last weekend. Example:
B: *I bought some tickets for a concert.*
A: *because I like going to the theatre.* (*I bought some tickets for a play because I like going to the theatre.*)

3 I was cleaning the house while my brother was . . .

Link words for time

1 Work in pairs. Compare what you and a member of your family (or a neighbour, flatmate or friend) were doing at the same time yesterday. Use these link words to do with time: *while, when, as, just as.* Examples:
I was practising the guitar while my sister was doing her homework.
When I was shopping, I saw George getting on a bus.
As I was leaving the flat, my mother came home from work.
Just as I was writing to her, Julia phoned from America.

2 Work as a class. Say your sentences to the class. Write down any interesting sentences that other people in the class say.

B Grammar guide

1 The *and* type of link word

- We can use *and* to put two actions together (= to link two actions), or to put nouns or adjectives together.
  I went home and watched television. (actions)
- *Also* means the same as *and.* We can use it with verbs, or to put two sentences together.
  I need a hammer; I also need a saw. (verbs)
  He doesn't talk to her and never helps with the housework. Also, he isn't interested in the children. (two sentences)
- If two sentences are negative, we can link them together with *not . . . either*, or *neither . . . nor* (but not with *also*).
  He's not a good husband. He's not a good father either.
  He is neither a good husband nor a good father.
- If there is a choice of two, you can use *either . . . or.*
  We can take either your blue suit or the brown one on holiday.
- We can use *or* with a choice of two or more. If there are more than two possibilities, *or* usually goes between the last two.
  We can have the party on Monday, Tuesday or Wednesday.

2 The *but* type of link word

- Use *but* when you are saying something different to what you said before.
  I need a hammer but I don't need a saw.
- *Although* means that there were good reasons for something not to happen, but it still happened.
  Andy came to the party, although I told him not to.
- *Unless* means something will happen if something else does not stop it.
  They should arrive at six, unless there is snow on the roads.

3 Cause and result link words

- We use *because* or *because of* to say why something happened (its cause).
  We didn't go out because it was raining.
  We didn't go out because of the rain.
- We use *so* to talk about the result of something.
  Gemma has a motorbike now, so she can travel more.

4 Link words for time

- We use *while* or *as* for two actions happening at the same time.
  I was doing the shopping while she was having a rest.
  That car hit the other one as I was coming out of the shop.
- When two actions happen at the same time and we want to emphasize that they happened together, we use *just as.*
  That car hit the other one just as I was coming out of the shop.
- We use *as soon as* to talk about one thing happening immediately after something else.
  You can go as soon as you've finished. (future)
  I came as soon as I heard the news. (past)
- We use *when* for the time something happened or will happen.
  Daniel looked fine when I saw him. (past)
  I'll give Joanne your message when I see her next week. (future)
  NOTE We use the present tense (*I see*) after *when* to talk about future time.

C Activities

1 Caroline: Part 1

Link words for cause, result and time

1 Work as a class. Make sure you understand this information. Some of the people in the class are sharing a flat with Caroline. Caroline seems to have led a very adventurous and interesting life. She is always telling you about the things she has done in the past, the jobs she has had, her successes, the exciting places she has lived in. But then you start to put all the stories together. You realize that Caroline is only a young woman. If she had really done everything she says, she would be much older. She is not telling the truth.

2 Work in pairs or small groups.

a What are all the things Caroline says she has done? Use the pictures in Activity note 71 on page 160 to give you ideas, but think of as many of your own ideas as you can, as well. Use as many of these link words to do with time as you realistically can: *while, as soon as, when, as, just as.*
Example: *She said she was a dancer when she was fifteen.*

b Why did she always go on to something new? Use these cause and result link words: *because, so, because of.*
Example: *She says she stopped being a rock singer because the band broke up.*

2 Caroline: Part 2

***and* and *but* type link words**

Work in pairs or small groups. One day Caroline suddenly disappears from the flat. What do you think she is doing now? Use as many of these *and* type of link words as you realistically can: *and, also, either . . . or, or, neither . . . nor, not . . . either.* Use these *but* type of link words: *but, unless, although.*
Example: *She may be singing with another band, although she can't sing very well.*

3 Coffee with Mr Fleming

Link words

Work in pairs or groups. Make sure that you understand the story below. Then write the story as a dialogue between you, your friend, the café owner and Mr Fleming. Each speech in the dialogue must have at least one link word in it. If you want to, a group of four can say or act your dialogue to the class, when you have finished it.
Example:
MARIA: *Look at that man. He looks nervous **and** odd.*
JULIA: *He **also** seems to be waiting for someone.*

You were sitting in your local café, having a coffee with a friend. At a nearby table there was a man who was obviously waiting for someone who had not turned up.

On the way out of the café you and your friend noticed a small packet on the floor. The man had dropped it. He had gone. You gave the packet to the café owner, who said that the man lived nearby. You decided to take the packet to his house.

The man, Mr Fleming, was grateful for the return of his packet and invited you and your friend into his house. He offered you something to eat and drink. He obviously didn't want you to leave and said he had a job for you both which would earn you a lot of money. He also clearly wanted to know if you had looked into the packet, but he didn't like to ask directly. He said the packet contained industrial diamonds.

It was late. You and your friend had been at the house for hours. Mr Fleming was playing chess with your friend. You passed the open door of Mr Fleming's study. He had torn the packet open and it was lying on his desk. It contained a white powder.

You went into the study and phoned the police. Mr Fleming was still playing chess when the police arrived and arrested him for drug dealing.

D Accuracy practice

1 Put in the correct *and* type of link word in these sentences.
Use: *and, also, either* (×2), *neither . . . nor, or, either . . . or.*

Example: Tom ___ his father both like fish.
Tom and his father both like fish.

1 Linda seems bored ___ fed up.
2 Vicky isn't very good at Spanish. She isn't good at French ___. She doesn't like languages.
3 Brenda often helps Paul with the washing up. She ___ repairs the car sometimes. They believe in sharing work.
4 ___ Bob ___ his father like fish. They both prefer meat.
5 The Andersons aren't coming and Jean and John Dixon aren't ___.
6 You can use the computer at ___ three o'clock ___ five o'clock but not at both times.
7 We can tell Matthew the bad news now ___ later.

2 Put in the correct *but* type of link word.
Use: *but, although, unless.*

1 I have to go to the meeting, ___ you don't.
2 Rachel kept playing, ___ she had hurt her arm quite badly.
3 We'll have the picnic tomorrow, ___ Rebecca has to go in to the office to do some extra work.

3 Make sentences by matching the two columns and putting in the missing cause or result type of link word in the right place. Use: *because, because of, so.*

1	We have no money	a	the rain.
2	The football match was cancelled	b	he had met another girl.
3	Jim told Sally he didn't want to see her any more	c	they can go a long time without water.
4	Camels manage well in the desert	d	we can't buy your mother a present.

4 Put in the missing link words for time. There is sometimes more than one possibility. Use: *while, just as, as soon as, when* (×2).

1 I'm very busy at the moment, but I'll speak to you I've finished talking to this lady.
2 It was amazing. Diane caught the vase it fell off the shelf.
3 I can be chopping the meat you are getting the vegetables ready.
4 I can't believe it. Claire and Jason were happily married I saw them last.
5 Please tell Joanna to come half an hour earlier than usual, you see her next week.

32

Some common grammar problems: the possessive; present perfect or present simple?; word order

A Starting activities

1 Envy

The possessive with *'s*

Work as a class. Say a possession or characteristic of someone else in the class that you wish you had. Use the possessive with *'s*.
Examples:
(possession) *I wish I had Miss Jones's car.*
(characteristic) *I wish I had Maria's intelligence.*

2 Someone new

Present perfect or present simple?

1 Work in pairs. Someone new has just come to the town where you are learning English. (Think of a real person, if you want to.) Write present perfect or present perfect progressive sentences with *for* or *since* which the new person would use to say what she or he has done, or has been doing, since arriving in your town. Then write present simple sentences which the new person would use to say something about her/himself. Examples:
(present perfect) *I've been to three discos since I arrived.*
(present perfect progressive) *I've been staying with friends for the last three weeks.*
(present simple) *I come from Japan. I don't like coffee.*

2 Work as a class. Read your sentences to the other people in the class. Listen to other people's sentences and list any interesting ones. Decide whose new person you would most like to meet.

3 Word order game

Word order

Work as a class. The class is in two teams, A and B. Your teacher will say a whole sentence to Team A and then point to somebody in the team. That person says the first word only of the sentence the teacher said. The next person the teacher points to in Team A says the second word (only) of the sentence and so on. The teacher can point to the same person in Team A more than once if she or he wishes to. If anyone in Team A hesitates or says the wrong word, Team B gets a chance at the same sentence. When a team repeats the sentence correctly it gets a point and the teacher says another sentence, to Team B this time. Your teacher will decide how long the game lasts.
Example: Teacher: *You left it on its side under the table last Monday.*
Person 1 from Team A: *You*
Person 2 from Team A: *left* (and so on)

NOTE TO TEACHER: Invent some sentences, or use sentences from this book or from a novel, magazine, newspaper etc. Make the sentences as hard or as easy as you like.

B Grammar guide

1 The possessive

- The possessive with *'s* is formed like this:
  Tom's bicycle (singular) *The Robinsons' car* (plural)
  It is used when something belongs to, or relates to, someone or something else. We use the possessive with *'s* to talk about:

a animate (living) things (e.g. people, animals): *the committee's decision, goat's milk*
b places: *London's biggest cinema.*
c time: *yesterday's paper, next week's timetable*
  But if there is a number in the expression, use two nouns: *a forty-minute lesson, a ten-minute wait*
d shops: *the butcher's, the newsagent's*

- The possessive with *of* means the same as the possessive with *'s* but we use it to talk about:

a expressions of quantity: *a loaf of bread*
b full containers: *a cup of coffee* (= a cup with coffee in it)
c inanimate things (e.g. houses, cars): *the roof of the house, the boot of the car*

- Don't use *'s* when talking about types of things.
  I must buy some cat food. (a type of food that is made for cats)
  BUT *This is the cat's food.* (some food that belongs to one particular cat)
  Also: *a wine bottle* (= a type of bottle), *a coffee cup* (a type of cup), *a garden chair, a car door*

2 The present perfect or the present simple

The most important point of contrast between these two tenses is that the present perfect describes the past until now and the present simple is used when the speaker thinks of something as a fact.

a *I have lived here for six years.* (present perfect)
b *I live here.* (present simple)

In (a) the action started six years ago and continues until now. In (b) the action is timeless and has no start or finish.

3 Word order

English usually has this word order:
subject–verb–object–manner (how?)–place (where?)–time (when?).
Smith scored a goal with his left foot at the match yesterday.
Possible variants include:

- Putting the time first.
  Yesterday I went to London.
- *There is/are* (or *there was/were* in the past) to show the existence or non-existence of something.
  There is a good story about that man.
  By the time I got to the baker's there were no cakes left.
- Impersonal *it* (*it is, it was* or *it will be*).
  It's raining. *It was Tim who fell.* *It will be fine tomorrow.*

C Activities

1 Conversations

The possessive

Work in pairs. Decide who is A and who is B. You are going to hold conversations on the three topics below. Change partners between each conversation so that you talk to three different people altogether. Make sure there is always an A and a B in each pair. Before you start, read the Activity notes.

Person A: Read Activity note 41 on page 148.
Person B: Read Activity note 56 on page 154.

Conversation 1: Persuasion
A and B are going on holiday together. A wants a quiet holiday near the sea. B wants a more active, exciting holiday in the mountains. Use specific holiday places that you know and can describe, if you want to.

Conversation 2: Argument
A borrowed some money from B. (How much? And what was the money borrowed for?) B says that A only paid some of it back. (When?) A says that she or he paid all of it back. (When?) Find a friendly solution to the disagreement.

Conversation 3: Co-operation
The place where you are studying English has been damaged by a storm and you want to help. List all the work that needs to be done and discuss what you and the class can do to help to put things right.

2 Parole board

Present perfect or present simple?

1 Work as a class. Make sure you know this crime vocabulary: *murder, armed robbery, blackmail, sentence, cell, prison, warder, prisoner, visitor, release (from prison).*

Three prisoners have applied to be released on parole. (That is, they have asked to be let out of prison for a short time before their permanent release.) Decide on the names, ages and crimes of the three prisoners then write questions that the parole board could ask the three prisoners. The questions should be about their behaviour in prison and about the reasons why they have asked to be released on parole. All the questions must be present perfect, present perfect progressive or present simple. Examples:
How long have you been a model prisoner?
Do you help in the prison library every day?

2 Work in pairs or groups. If you are in pairs, one of you is one of the prisoners and the other person is a member of the parole board. If you are in groups, there are three prisoners and three parole board groups. Each prisoner goes to all three parole board groups in turn, to be interviewed. Using the questions from part 1 to help you (but adding new questions too) the parole board asks the prisoners why they should be released on parole. If you are working in groups and you are interviewing more than one prisoner, choose the best one to release on parole.

3 The wild thing from the woods

Word order

Work in pairs. The 'wild thing from the woods' grew up alone in the forest but is now learning to live in an English town. He or she can say only two words at a time. Each of these two words is from one of these categories: subject, verb, object, manner, place and time. For example, the 'wild thing' can say *I go* (subject, verb) or *go quietly* (verb, manner) or *him tomorrow* (object, time). Take it in turns to be 'the wild thing'. Say two words, one from each category. The other person completes the 'wild thing's' sentence. Example:
A (wild thing): *I carefully* (subject, manner)
B: *I will cross the road carefully.*

D Accuracy practice

1 Make possessive sentences with *'s, of* or two nouns together. More than one answer is sometimes possible.

1 Don't shut the door yet. (car)
2 The football match is the last of the season. (Saturday)
3 There's some bread on the table. (loaf)
4 Put it in the room, would you, please. (corner)
5 Can you wash the cups up, please? (coffee)
6 Would you like an orange juice? (glass)

2 Change the present perfect sentences to present simple and the present simple sentences to present perfect using the words in brackets.

1 I am a Beatles fan. (since I was twelve)
2 She doesn't like rock music. (never)
3 Do you ever go to the cinema? (a late-night cinema show)
4 We haven't seen her for ages. (much these days)
5 Have you ever had any serious health problems? (at the moment)

3 Put in *there is/are, there was/were* or *it is/was/will be.*

1 Look, ____ raining.
2 ____ a good film on next week.
3 ____ a rainy day in October when it happened.
4 ____ a notice about that on the noticeboard last week.
5 ____ four things you must try not to forget, but ____ a miracle if you remember them all.

4 These sentences are from a holiday postcard from Niki to her brother Ben. Complete them by putting the words in the right order.

1 We are having ____________
time a really here at the moment great
2 The weather has been brilliant, though ____________
some clouds there in the sky were today
3 The hotel is not too bad, but ____________
there are too many tourists and fed up are getting the staff
4 The food, however, ____________
is good exceptionally
5 Tomorrow we hope to go ____________
and on a trip organized the local sights some by the hotel of see

Activity notes

1 **Wrong!**

[page 8]
Person A

1 Say these wrong 'facts' to your partner (B), who will correct you.
   1 Water freezes at five degrees centigrade.
   2 The President of the United States lives in New York.
   3 Water floats on oil.
   4 Boris Becker plays football.
   5 The capital of Italy is Milan.

   Start the activity as soon as you and B are ready.

2 Your partner (B) will say some facts that are wrong. Correct B using emphatic *do/does*. (Example: *No, he doesn't like beef. He's a vegetarian.*) The information you need to correct B is below.
   6 The earth goes round the sun.
   7 The capital of Britain is London.
   8 The Swedish flag is blue and yellow.
   9 Water boils at a hundred degrees centigrade.
   10 A rose is a kind of flower.

2 **Sack Mr Smith?**

[page 10]
Person A

Discuss this information from a report about Mr Smith with your partner (B) and listen to what B has to say about his or her report. Use emphatic *do/does* sentences where you can. Decide whether or not the firm should sack Mr Smith.

Information from a report on Reginald Smith by Jane Pettifer, Head of Personnel

- Late for work quite often.
- Not always polite. Can be rude if he has 'had a bad day'.
- Regularly misses monthly meetings with me.
- Smokes in the sales office, even when asked not to.
- Has occasionally missed appointments and does not always ring to apologize.
- Sales are not particularly good.

3 **Some questions**

[page 20]

1 a I had not finished lunch in sentence 1. (past progressive)
   b I had finished lunch in sentence 2. (past simple)

2 a Past simple
   b Yes

3 The speaker sees the accident happening as the most important action and driving to London as the background, less important, action.

4 Windows

[page 10]
Person A

1 Describe these pictures to your partner (B). You can describe the pictures as many times as B wants you to.

2 Listen to B's description of two pictures and try to remember exactly what B says about them. Take notes if you need to.

5 Which is used when?

[page 8]

1 e Permanent situation (present simple)
2 c Temporary situation (present progressive)
3 d Law of nature (present simple)
4 b Changing or developing situation (present progressive)
5 f Regular repeated action (present simple)
6 a Action still happening (present progressive)

6 Some funny things happened

[page 22]
Person A

You want to describe what happened when you were in the shop with B. Write the first half of four sentences. Use *just* and the past progressive. Example: *I was just buying some bread . . .*

Use these ideas or your own ideas:
(get) change from the assistant
(go) through the checkout
(choose) a nice . . . as a present for . . .

Tell B your incomplete sentences (one at a time) when B is ready. B will finish each sentence for you.

7 Cinderella, all wrong

[page 20]

Cinderella was a young woman who lived with her stepmother and her two ugly sisters. Cinderella had to do all the work around the house. She went around in rags while her two sisters wore beautiful clothes. One day there was a ball at the prince's palace and a beautiful fairy godmother appeared and told Cinderella that she could go to the ball – but she had to be back by midnight. So Cinderella went to the ball and danced with the handsome prince. As she left she dropped her glass slipper on the stairs. The next day the prince searched everywhere for Cinderella and when he found her he married her.

8 Looking after Harry

[page 34]
Person A

You are, of course, very worried about Harry after your day out. Write down as many present perfect and past simple questions about Harry's day as you can. Examples:
Has he eaten anything?
Did he play with the girl next door?

If you get just a short answer in reply, for example *Yes, he has* or *No, he didn't*, ask for more details with more present perfect and past simple questions.

NOTE Actually, you don't think B looks after children very well. You can say so if you like, but nicely. Start when you are both ready.

9 Drawing time lines

[page 32]

Numbers 1, 3 and 4 are present perfect.

Present perfect
PAST NOW

Numbers 2 and 5 are past simple.

Past simple
PAST NOW

10 A new plan for the club

[page 46]
Person A

Imagine you are walking round the club, listing problems. List each problem using the present perfect progressive. There are some problems below but try to use your own ideas too.
Example: *Somebody has been damaging the table tennis tables.*

Problems
table tennis tables damaged
people get into the discos without paying
some members take cassettes and CDs
members take drinks from the bar without paying
Assistant Manager leaves without locking up

B has a list of some more problems. When you and B are ready, listen to B's problems and try to find a solution for each of them. Then tell B the problems you have listed and discuss B's solutions.

11 What happened first?

[page 56]

1
- a
  1. we had fallen in love
  2. we got married
- b
  1. someone had broken into my flat
  2. I got home
- c
  1. he had just drunk four glasses of wine
  2. he crashed the car
- d
  1. the film had started
  2. we arrived at the cinema
- e
  1. they had eaten all the cake
  2. I got home

2 The past perfect is used for the first action.

12 An insurance claim

[page 58]
Person A

B does not want to pay you any money on your insurance claim. Persuade her/him. Be ready to answer these questions.

The food poisoning (Day two of the holiday)
In the evening your wife/husband was ill. You had both had lunch at a nice little restaurant, near the beach.

- What had you both eaten?
- Had you been eating shellfish on holiday?
- Had you been drinking the local wine?
- After you had eaten the meal, how long was it before your wife/husband began to feel ill?

The car crash (Day three of the holiday)
You crashed the car on a pretty mountain road.

- How long had you been driving before the crash?
- Had you had anything at all to drink?
- Had you ever driven this make of car before? (Which make was it? A Ford? A Volkswagen? A Citroën?)

The robbery from the hotel room (Day four of the holiday)
During the day your hotel room was robbed.

- Had you locked the door when you went out?
- Had you handed the key in at reception?
- Had you been sunbathing on the beach for long?

B will start when you are ready.

13 She's leaving home

[page 78]
Person A

You are a parent. Your son or daughter (B) is leaving home for the first time. B is, of course, much too young for something like this. You are, of course, worried. Ask B questions about his or her future life using the present progressive for future time, *will* and *going to*.
Examples:
Are you going to look for a flat?
Will you stay near here, or move away?

When you and B are ready, start asking your questions and have a conversation about B's future life.

14 This time next week

[page 100]

Future progressive

1. I'll be lying . . .
2. I'll be working . . .
3. I'll be staying . . .
4. I'll be thinking . . .
5. I'll be meeting . . .
6. I'll be having dinner . . .
7. I'll be going up . . .

Future perfect

1. Will you have typed . . .?
2. I'll have finished . . .
3. You won't have done . . .

15 Which is which? II

[page 80]

Past time

Negative possibility: *He may/might not have gone to London.*
Possibility, question: *Might/could he have gone to London?*
Positive probability: *He should/ought to have gone to London.*
Positive deduction: *He must have gone to London.*
Negative deduction: *He can't/couldn't have gone to London.*

16 Well, just a few friends perhaps

[page 50]
Person A

There are several things you want to do while your parents are away. Ask your parent (B). Examples:
Can I use your computer?
Would you mind giving me all the keys?

Here are some ideas, but you can add more of your own:

You want to have a big party and invite all your friends.
You want to borrow your parents' car. (You have a friend of eighteen who has a driving licence.)
You want your parents to leave their weekend address and telephone number.
You want your parents to leave you a spare key.
You want to start repainting your bedroom. (Your friends will help.)
You want to do some babysitting for a couple who live twenty miles away.

Your parents have some requests for you too. You start the conversation when B is ready.

17 Getting them clear

[page 12]

1. Offer, formal
2. Asking for advice, informal
3. Suggestion, informal
4. Offer, informal
5. Suggestion, informal

18 Homeless

[page 14]
Person A

It is the middle of the night. You and your family (your wife/husband, your father and your two children) are homeless. Think of the advice and help you need. What questions will you ask when people offer you help? Make a list, like this:
How shall we keep the baby warm?
What shall we do about getting food?

B is the representative of a group of neighbours who want to help you. Ask B for advice, using your list of questions where you can. You start when B is ready.

19 Why are these wrong?

[page 24]

1 c
2 b
3 e

20 He gave up hope

[page 88]

a Prices are going up.
b He gave up hope.
c The government will put taxes up.
d I grew up in London.
e Do that parcel up, please.
f He was brought up by his grandparents.
g School breaks up in June.
h Let's load the car up.
i It's time to wrap the presents up.
j They beat him up.
k Shut up! (not polite).
l Sit by the fire and warm up.
m She looks unhappy. Let's cheer her up.
n Zip your dress up.
o Turn the sound up.
p The hotel is booked up.
q Clean the room up.
r Fold your clothes up and put them away.

21 She made a complete fool of herself

[page 108]

You can add anything you like after these sentences to explain what happened.

1 (i) He made a complete fool of himself in the lesson.
(ii) What she told me was absolute nonsense.
(iii) Everything we did was a total waste of time.

2 (i) She totally disagreed and said he should apologize.
(ii) She is absolutely right about Shane's birthday.
(iii) He completely wasted the opportunity.

22 Evelyn and Les

[page 120]
Person A

You have the first line of the dialogue. Wait for B's reply before you say the next line.

EVELYN	I saw Bob yesterday.
LES	. . .
EVELYN	Bob lives in London now.
LES	. . .
EVELYN	Yes. Helen and Bob have had separate houses for years. They just see each other at weekends.
LES	. . .
EVELYN	That's interesting. Tim was Helen's first husband, you know.

When you and B have said the dialogue, put it into indirect speech, working together.

23 He said, she said

[page 120]

1 said
2 thought
3 suggested
4 warned
5 advised
6 replied/said

24 Drugs kill

[page 122]

Mr and Mrs Roper disapprove of Sheena's new boyfriend. They and Sheena's younger brother, Gary, think that he sells drugs at the local café.

MR ROPER	You are not to see him again. Am I making myself clear, girl? You must stay at home and never see him again.
SHEENA	I can go out if I want to.
MR ROPER	He's like all the rest of them at that café. They sell drugs there, I tell you.
MRS ROPER	The café's not so bad in the afternoons. It's in the evenings that they come in . . . those . . . those people who sell the drugs. Those pushers.
GARY	He is definitely on drugs, Mum. Maybe he's even a pusher himself.
SHEENA	Oh, thank you, little brother, thank you very much. You're just jealous, aren't you? And all because Mum and Dad made you leave school and go to work so I could try to get to university. Well, that's not my fault. It wasn't my idea and anyway I'm more likely to get to university than you are.
GARY	You were more likely, you mean. Before you met him and started going to places like the café and started . . .
SHEENA	Shut up, Gary.
MRS ROPER	Oh, Sheena, you don't take drugs. Oh, no!
GARY	Drugs kill you, big sister. You just remember that.

25 Starting off

[page 108]

1 Stronger: *really, absolute*
Weaker: *fairly*

26 Starting off

[page 108]

2 (i) She's an absolute beginner at English.
(ii) He's a fairly good guitarist.
(iii) I really enjoy going to the theatre.

27 How many combinations do you know?

[page 68]

Grid 1	get	go	make	do
off	✓	✓	✓	×
back	✓	✓	×	×
up	✓	✓	✓	✓

Grid 2	come	take	go	make
up	✓	✓	✓	✓
in	✓	✓	✓	×
to	✓	✓	✓	×

Grid 3	take	put	do	get
to	✓	×	✓	✓
back	✓	✓	×	✓
up	✓	✓	✓	✓

NOTE Where the phrasal verb has more than one meaning, only the most common is given here.

come in become fashionable. *I hope short skirts don't come in again this summer.*

come to regain consciousness (e.g. after fainting). *She came to and asked what had happened.*

come up be mentioned or discussed. *If salaries come up at the meeting, what shall I say?*

do to have an effect on someone. *If you don't come, Jim will be upset. Don't do that to him.*

do up fasten. *This dress does up at the back.*

get back arrive at the place where you started from. *We got back home from the party at midnight.*

get off remove. *I can't get the top off this jar.*

get to annoy. *That loud music's really getting to me. Turn it down, please.*

get up get out of bed in the morning. *The alarm wakes me up at seven-thirty and I get up at about seven forty-five.*

go back return to. *Last year we went back to Tokyo for the first time in ten years.*

go in (sun or moon) be hidden behind a cloud. *It's quite cold now that the sun's gone in.*

go off go bad (used for meat, fruit and dairy products like milk and cheese but not for bread). *We've had the cheese for a week now and it's gone off.*

go to be given to someone. *First prize goes to Michael Adams!*

go up be built. *There are some new houses going up in the village.*

make off go away quickly. *When I shouted at the door-to-door salesman he made off down the road.*

make up say something that is not true. *He made up a story to explain why he was driving someone else's car.* ▶

put back return an object to where it was. *I put that book of yours back on the shelf where I found it.*
put up give someone a place to sleep for a limited time. *We can put you up whenever you are in Oxford.*
take back return something (to a shop or a public building). *I took your library books back to the library for you.*
take in deceive. *I thought he was a nice person but he isn't. The smile and the charm took me in completely.*
take to get to like people or places. *I've never taken to Bath. There are too many tourists and there's too much traffic.*
take up start a new hobby or start learning a new musical instrument. *I took up fishing last year and I go fishing regularly now.*

---

28 I must dash off

[page 88]

Group 1: a, d, e
Group 2: h
Group 3: b, g
Group 4: c, f

The phrasal verb which does not fit into a group: i.

---

29 What follows?

[page 104]

1

verb + *-ing*	verb + infinitive	verb + infinitive without *to*
risk	want	should
avoid	promise	would rather
keep on	offer	ought to
suggest	refuse	
postpone	tend	
deny		

---

30 Kids!

[page 30]
Person A

Write five statements or opinions about children. Make some of the statements negative and some positive. Add a question tag asking for agreement to each one.
Example: *Children aren't difficult to look after, are they?*

B is also writing five statements about children. Agree or disagree with each of B's statements. Example:
B: *Children make a lot of noise, don't they?*
A: *Yes, they do.* (OR *No, they don't.*)

Say your five statements to B when you are ready. Stop after each statement to give B time to speak. Then listen and reply to B's statements. You start this activity.

31 This is about question tags, isn't it?

[page 28]

1. It's a nice day, isn't it? (Example)
2. The supermarket sells newspapers, doesn't it?
3. I'm late, aren't I?
4. Tom doesn't like soup, does he? OR
   You don't like soup, do you (Tom)?
5. Diane has read 'War and Peace', hasn't she? OR
   You have read 'War and Peace', haven't you (Diane)?
6. Dick and Tina went camping last year, didn't they? OR
   You did go camping last year, didn't you?
7. Old Mrs Pearson hasn't been well lately, has she? OR
   You haven't been well lately, have you (Mrs Pearson)?
8. Margaret isn't playing tennis tomorrow, is she? OR
   You're not playing tennis tomorrow, are you (Margaret)?
9. Dick wasn't there when Joy came, was he? OR
   You weren't there when Joy came, were you Dick?
10. Mr Sanders hasn't been telling the truth, has he? OR
    You haven't been telling the truth, have you (Mr Sanders)?

32 Brainstorming

[page 88]

Here are some phrasal verbs with the adverb particles *down, in, off, out* and *up*. There are more in the Grammar guide.

down

sit down　　write down　　knock down
bring down (prices, inflation, taxes)　　turn down (= say 'no' to)

in

break in (= force a way in)　　stay/wait in (for someone or something)

off

pair off (= separate into pairs)　　chop off (a branch from a tree)
put off (= postpone)　　cut off (water, electricity, telephone)
wear off (= get less intense, fade)

out

break out (of prison)　　die out (species of animals or plants)
give/hand out (= distribute)　　work out (the answer)
call out　　write out
show someone out (= take them outside)

up

eat up (= eat all of)　　load up (cars, vans, lorries)
speak up (= speak more loudly)　　fill up (with petrol)
cheer up (= get more cheerful)

33 Have you made any progress?

[page 40]

The countable nouns are: book, football match, cupboard.

34 What follows?

[page 104]

2 The difference in meaning:
forget + infinitive is 'before the action'.
forget + *-ing* is 'after the action'.
remember + infinitive is 'before the action'.
remember + *-ing* is 'after the action'.
stop + infinitive gives the reason for stopping.
stop + *-ing* gives the action which ended.

35 A look at the system

[page 64]

1 **Group 1:** a, c and f have the comparative *-er* and the superlative *-est.* (a and c because they are one-syllable adjectives. f is a two-syllable adjective ending in *-y.*)
Group 2: b, d and e have the comparative *more* and superlative *the most.* (b and d because they are long adjectives. e because the adjective ends in *-ed.*)

2 a *than* b *as* c *the*

3 a *more often, most often*
b *earlier, earliest*
c *more smoothly, most smoothly*
d *longer, longest*
e *harder, hardest*

36 After the party

[page 16]
Person A

It is after the party. A lot of things have been left behind in the living room by your friends. (See the list of objects below.) Explain to your mother or father, using the phrases below plus prepositions of position and movement, exactly where the objects are in the living room and how they got there.
Example: *You see that pair of socks under the round table? I'm afraid somebody decided to dance barefoot and he took off his socks and forgot about them.*

Phrases:
You see that . . .
I'm afraid there's a . . .
I'm sorry, but that . . .

Objects: a bicycle, a parrot in a cage, a large cake, a diamond ring, a pair of football boots, a London telephone directory, a rubber duck

Start the activity as soon as you are both ready. Either of you can start.

37 Every picture tells a story

[page 18]

NOTE *This text is for the teacher only.*

There is a house in the bottom left-hand corner of the picture. The house has four windows. In the house, there is a woman at the window at the top, on the left. She's waving. A man is just going into the house. He is actually at the door with the key in his hand. There is a bird on the roof of the house. Another bird is just flying off. It is just above the roof of the house. There is also a river in the picture. It runs from the top right-hand corner to the bottom left-hand corner, by the house. There is a bridge over the river. A man is walking over the bridge and there is a small dog running along beside him. Under the bridge, there is a child in the river. The child is shouting, 'Help, I'm drowning'.

38 Preposition grids

[page 112]

NOTE The three grids show which prepositions combine with the listed verbs, adjectives and nouns. The answers do not include any of the usual meanings of prepositions (like *at* for time) which can follow many verbs, adjectives or nouns. For example, *We **decided at** three o'clock* is correct but that preposition combination is not ticked in the grid.

Grid 1	of	for	with	about	at	on
laugh	×	×	×	✓	✓	×
decide	×	×	×	✓	×	✓
ask	×	✓	×	✓	×	×
negotiate	×	✓	✓	✓	×	✓
dream	✓	×	×	✓	×	×
worry	×	×	×	✓	×	×

Grid 2	at	with	by	of	to	about
fed up	×	✓	×	×	×	✓
surprised	✓	×	✓	×	×	✓
married	×	×	×	×	✓	×
nice	×	×	×	✓	✓	✓
amused	✓	×	✓	×	×	✓
bored	×	✓	✓	×	×	×

NOTE Grid 2 does not include idioms like *bored to tears*.
They were married by the vicar is correct but *married* is not an adjective here.

Grid 3	for	in	of	to	with
sympathy	✓	×	×	×	✓
photograph	×	×	✓	×	×
reaction	×	×	×	✓	×
exception	×	×	✓	✓	×
damage	×	×	×	✓	×
recipe	✓	×	×	×	×

39 The police are on the way

[page 40]

Singular verb: news, politics, economics, mathematics
Plural verb: police, people, clothes, pyjamas, shoes, trousers, glasses, scissors, goods, savings, premises

40 About relative clauses

[page 60]

1
1 who is sitting over there
2 which are in front of the entrance
3 whose favourite team lost the first six matches of the season
4 who gave you that information
5 that was cancelled
6 whose parents had once lived in the village
7 who had never been polite

2 Arthur Grimes, who is thirty, painted 'The Cherry Tree'.

41 Conversations

[page 134]
Person A

Use as many of these phrases as you can in your conversations with B.

1 **Persuasion**
Some of Britain's most beautiful scenery (or any other country or area)
Last night's news
The front of the hotel
A glass of wine (or any other drink)

2 **Argument**
At least half of the money (or any other amount)
Today's expenses
A three-week wait (or any other length of time)
My telephone bill

3 **Co-operation**
The side of the building
Next week's lesson
A pane of glass
With our teacher's help

42 Wrong!

[page 8]
Person B

1 Your partner (A) will say some facts that are wrong. Correct A using emphatic *do/does*. (Example: *No, he doesn't like beef. He's a vegetarian.*) The information you need to correct A is below.
1 Water freezes at nought degrees centigrade.
2 The President of the United States lives in Washington.
3 Oil floats on water.
4 Boris Becker plays tennis.
5 The capital of Italy is Rome.

A will start the activity when you are ready.

2 Say these wrong 'facts' to your partner. A will correct you.
6 The sun goes round the earth.
7 The capital of Britain is Birmingham.
8 The Swedish flag is red and white.
9 Water boils at two hundred degrees centigrade.
10 A rose is a kind of tree.

43 Sack Mr Smith?

[page 10]
Person B

Discuss this information from a report about Mr Smith with your partner (A) and listen to what A has to say about his or her report. Use emphatic *do/does* sentences where you can. Decide whether or not the firm should sack Mr Smith.

Information from a report on Reginald Smith by Jim Bowes, Head of Sales and Marketing.

- Sometimes late for work when his car breaks down.
- Usually polite and helpful.
- Thinks monthly meetings with Head of Personnel are not helpful.
- Sometimes misses appointments but rings to apologize.
- Has a lot of supermarkets to visit.
- Sales are about average for the time of year.

44 Some funny things happened

[page 22]
Person B

You want to describe what happened when you were in the shop with A. A is writing the first half of four sentences using *just* and the past progressive. For example, *I was just buying some bread.* Write the second half of four sentences saying what happened. Use the past simple and begin with *when.*

Use these ideas or your own ideas:
. . . when the assistant (scream)
. . . when the ceiling (fall in)
. . . when the manager (come up) to me and (say) . . .

When A gives you the beginnings of the four sentences (one at a time) you add one of your four endings. Choose the ending which you think makes the most interesting sentence each time.

45 An interview

[page 22]

Notes about famous people

MOTHER TERESA (AGNES GONXHA BOJAXHIU) (Nun and helper of the poor)
Born 1910 in Skopje (Yugoslavia)

1928	Became a nun
1950	Founded the Congregation of the Missionaries of Charity in Calcutta. She resigned as its head in 1990 but was re-elected later the same year. She has set up more than fifty schools, orphanages and houses for the poor in India and in other countries.
1952	Founded the Pure Heart Home for Dying Destitutes (a hospice)
1964	Started a leper colony in West Bengal
1971	Was awarded the Pope John XXIII Peace Prize
1975	Wrote *Gift for God*, a book about her work
1979	Won the Nobel Peace Prize

▶

PAUL McCARTNEY (Singer, songwriter and former member of *The Beatles*)
Born 1942 in Liverpool (England)

1957–9	Played with John Lennon in a group called *The Quarrymen*
1960	(December) First appearance of *The Beatles* at Litherland Town Hall
1963	*The Beatles* played for the Queen at the Royal Variety Performance
1964	*The Beatles'* coast-to-coast tour of the USA was a huge success. *The Beatles* were the first British group to be really successful in America.
1969	Married Linda Eastman. All Paul and Linda's children went to state schools, not private schools.
1970	*The Beatles* disbanded (last public performance, January 1969)
1971	Started a new group called *Wings*
1972–3	Tour of Europe with *Wings*
1981	*Wings* disbanded

Some of the albums *The Beatles* made between 1959 and 1969 were: *Rubber Soul* (1965), *Sergeant Pepper's Lonely Hearts Club Band* (1967), *The Beatles* (1968). Some of the albums Paul released as a solo artist and with *Wings* were: *McCartney* (1970), *Band on the Run* (1973) and *McCartney II* (1980).

Paul also wrote the music for the film *The Family Way* (1967) and the title song for the James Bond film *Live and Let Die* (1973).

HER MAJESTY QUEEN ELIZABETH II (Queen of Great Britain and Northern Ireland)
Born 1926 in London (England)

1953	Crowned as Queen
1947	Married His Royal Highness Prince Philip, Duke of Edinburgh
1948	Prince Charles was born. His Investiture (crowning) as Prince of Wales was in 1969.
1950	Princess Anne born
1960	Prince Andrew born
1964	Prince Edward born

The many Royal tours the Queen has made include Tonga (1953), Ghana (1961), New Zealand (1970) – which included the first Royal 'walkabout' – and the USA (1991). She was the first British monarch to speak in the American Congress building. The Queen's work includes a meeting with the Prime Minister every Tuesday. ▶

WALT DISNEY (Animator and founder of Disneyland)
Born 1901 in Chicago (USA)

1917–19 Ambulance driver in France in the First World War
1919 Joined a firm making animated films (cartoons) for advertisements in cinemas
1921 Started own company making animated fairy tales like *Cinderella, Goldilocks and the Three Bears* and *Jack and the Beanstalk.*
1923 Disney was the first to combine live action with a cartoon, using a real little girl to play Alice in *Alice in Wonderland.* All the other characters in the film were cartoons.
1928 First appearance of Mickey Mouse, in *Steamboat Willie* – one of the first 'talkies' and the first cartoon with sound
1932 *Flowers and Trees* – the first cartoon in full colour
1937 *Snow White* – one of the first full-length animated films
1940 Disney released *Pinocchio,* which many people consider was his best film

Other famous films followed, including *Bambi, Fantasia, Peter Pan, Robin Hood* and, in 1964, *Mary Poppins* (not a cartoon).

There are three Disney theme parks: Disneyland in Los Angeles (opened in 1955), Disneyworld in Florida (opened in 1971) and Eurodisney near Paris (opened in 1992).

BRIGITTE BARDOT (Film star and campaigner for animal rights)
Born 1934 in France

1952 Made her first film. (First job was as a model.) Her early films include *And God Created Woman* directed by her husband, Roger Vadim. Other early films include *Manina* and *Babette.*
1967 Made the film *Two Weeks in September*
1968 Made *Shalako,* which co-starred Sean Connery
1973 Made *Don Juan,* her last film

Brigitte Bardot has been married three times, to Roger Vadim, Jacques Charrier and Gunther Sachs. She has been single since 1969.

After she left the film industry, Brigitte devoted herself to animal rights. She started the Brigitte Bardot Foundation to help animals.

---

46 How long?

[page 56]

1 a (i) b (ii)
2 Past perfect progressive

47 Looking after Harry

[page 34]
Person B

You have looked after this ten-year-old monster all day and you are exhausted and angry. (To make yourself feel better, write down some adjectives that describe how you feel.)
Write down some past simple and present perfect sentences saying what Harry has done. Example:
He spat his dinner at the wall.
He's torn my jacket. Look at it!

If A asks questions about Harry, just give short answers (like *Yes, he has* or *No, he didn't*) and then tell A all your complaints about what Harry has done.

NOTE Actually you think that A should take Harry with her/him next time. Start when you are both ready.

48 Choose the rule

[page 44]

1 'Use the present perfect and not the present perfect progressive to talk about completed actions.' (i) explains why 1b is wrong.

2 'Use the present perfect progressive to describe actions in the recent past that you think have been happening because of something you can see now (present evidence).' (iv) explains why 2b is wrong.

49 A new plan for the club

[page 46]
Person B

Imagine you are walking round the club, listing problems. List each problem using the present perfect progressive. There are some problems below but try to use your own ideas too.
Example: *Somebody has been writing graffiti on the walls.*

Problems
graffiti on walls
a gang throw stones through windows
members don't pay monthly subscription
some members give beer and wine to under-age children
drugs sold at the club

A has a list of some more problems. When you and A are ready, tell A the problems you have listed and discuss A's solutions. Then listen to A's problems and try to find a solution for each of them.

50 An insurance claim

[page 58]
Person B

You are an insurance officer. Here are some questions for A and some things to say to her/him. You do not want to pay A's insurance claim. Tell A why not.

The food poisoning (Day two of A's holiday)

- The representative had warned Mr and Mrs A not to eat at the little restaurants near the beach. They are lucky to be alive.
- If Mr and Mrs A had been eating shellfish it is not surprising that one of them was ill. Had they been eating shellfish?
- Had they been drinking wine with the meal?
- When had A's wife/husband started to feel ill? ▶

The car crash (Day three of A's holiday)

- The police said A had been drinking before the car crash. Had A been drinking?
- Had A ever driven this make of car before?
- How long had A been driving before the crash?

The robbery from the hotel room (Day four of A's holiday)

- The hotel receptionist had told Mr and Mrs A, several times, not to go out without locking the room door.
- Mr and Mrs A had never handed their key in at reception, not once.
- Mr and Mrs A had lost their room key twice during the first two days of the holiday.
- How long had they been sunbathing on the beach?

You start when you and A are ready.

---

51 She's leaving home

[page 78]
Person B

You are a young person leaving home for the first time. Your parent (A) is worried about you, but you have plans and ideas. Tell A about your plans and ideas using the present progressive for future time, *will* and *going to.*
Examples:
I'm going to a job interview next week.
I'm moving in with a friend.

When you and A are ready, A will ask you some questions about your future life.

---

52 Which is which? I

[page 80]

Present and future time

Negative possibility: *He may/might not be in London.*
Possibility, question: *Could/might he be in London?*
Positive probability: *He should/ought to be in London now.*
Positive deduction: *He must be in London.*
Negative deduction: *He can't be in London.*

---

53 Sorting them out

[page 48]

1 Request, formal
2 Permission, informal
3 Permission, formal
4 Request, informal
5 Request, formal

54 Well, just a few friends perhaps

[page 50]
Person B

There are several things you want your fifteen-year-old child to do while you are away. Ask your child (A). Examples:
Will you lock all the doors when you go out, please?
Would you please buy some bread?

Here are some ideas, but you can add more of your own:
You want your daughter/son to water the plants.
You want her/him to feed the cat.
You don't want her/his boyfriend/girlfriend in the flat while you are away. (Anyway he/she is too old for your child.)
You want her/him to invite the old lady who lives next door over for coffee and cakes and to read to her for two or three hours.
You want her/him to wash the car and clean the house.
You want her/him to write some 'thank you' letters for birthday presents.

Your child has some requests for you too. A will start the conversation when you are ready.

55 Homeless

[page 14]
Person B

It is the middle of the night, A and his or her family are homeless. You are representing a group of three or four neighbours who have offered to help A after the disaster. Write down their names and what they have said they will do, like this:
Mrs Jones will put the family up for the night.

A will be asking for advice and help for his or her family. Listen to A and make offers of help. Where you can, use the sentences with *will* that you have written. When A asks for advice, answer with suggestions using *shall* with *I* or *we*. Example:
A: *How shall we keep the baby warm?*
B: *Shall I lend you this old coat for now?*

A will start when you are ready.

56 Conversations

[page 134]
Person B

Use as many of these phrases as you can in your conversations with A.

1 **Persuasion**
At the travel agent's
A four-hour delay
Julia's friend
At the top of the mountain

2 **Argument**
Some of the money
The newsagent's
My mother's friend
A four-week period (or any other length of time)

3 **Co-operation**
The caretaker's broom
John's friend (or any other name)
A tool kit
A cup of tea

57 Wrong turnings

[page 74]

Graham came from a very poor family. The love of his life was painting. He wanted to go to art college when he was nineteen but his parents said he should study law. He studied law but regretted it all his life. At university he did not do as much work as he should have done, as he still spent a lot of time painting. Half-way through his university course he met Davina. They fell in love. Davina wanted to wait until she had finished at university before they got married, but Graham persuaded her to get married immediately, so she did not finish studying. She always regretted that, especially as she was studying theatre, which she loved. Graham and Davina had a baby son while he was studying for his examinations. It was a difficult time. He failed his examinations and did not become a lawyer. He needed to get a job quickly so he went to work in the office of a friend he had been studying with the year before. Graham was an assistant to this friend, whose name was Clive. Graham never really liked that situation, and it made it worse when Clive offered to lend him some money for a flat, as by now Davina was expecting another baby. Later on Graham found out that Davina had asked Clive to lend them the money and he never forgave her for that. Their marriage never recovered from it. Graham wanted to leave Clive's office and go and paint on a desert island, like Gauguin, but he never did. He was against Davina going out to work or going back to university. However, she got a job as a typist and then got another job helping out in a theatre. Finally she applied to go to drama school in London and to her surprise got in. But this meant that Graham would have to look after the children.

58 Choices

[page 120]

All the indirect speech sentences (a and b) are correct. By choosing sentence (b) in each of the three pairs of sentences the speaker is emphasizing that what he or she is talking about is still true.

59 Evelyn and Les

[page 120]
Person B

Wait for A's line and then say your first line. Say each of your lines after A's.

EVELYN . . .
LES That's interesting. I saw Helen, Bob's wife.
EVELYN . . .
LES What? Helen doesn't live in London. She has a house in Brighton I think.
EVELYN . . .
LES Really? Helen was walking along with Tim.
EVELYN . . .

When you and B have said the dialogue put it into indirect speech, working together.

60 Active or passive?

[page 96]

1 active (A is talking about the Marconi family, so B mentions them first in his sentence. The new information, that they eat a lot of Italian food, comes second.)
2 passive (We often use the passive in formal notices. In this way we don't have to say who will do the action – in this case, prosecute.)
3 passive (A is talking about the car, so B mentions that first in his sentence. The new information, that it is being serviced, comes second.)

61 Sorting them out

[page 16]

in: position, movement, time
at: position, time
on: position, movement, time
onto: movement
into: movement
along: position, movement
during: time

62 He gave up hope

[page 88]

Person A: a, c, d, f, l, m, o mean 'getting bigger' or 'more' in some way.
Person B: b, e, g, i, j, k, n, p, q, r mean 'stopping' or finishing' or 'completing an action'.
h will go into both groups.

63 Story time

[page 90]

Grid 1	give	put	send	pull
back	✓	✓	✓	✓
off	✓	✓	✓	✓
down	×	✓	✓	✓
over	×	✓	✓	✓

Grid 2	break	take	fall	drive
on	×	✓	×	✓
up	✓	✓	×	✓
in	✓	✓	✓	✓
away	✓	✓	✓	✓

Grid 3	get	let	go	tear
through	✓	✓	✓	✓
out	✓	✓	✓	✓
up	✓	✓	✓	✓
about	✓	×	✓	✓

NOTE Not all the possible combinations are phrasal verbs. In these cases no definition has been given, only an example sentence.

give back return something. *Give that toy back to your sister at once.*

put back replace something. *Please put reference books back on the shelf when you have finished with them.*

send back return something through the post. *This shirt I ordered is the wrong size. I'll have to send it back.*

pull back cause to return. *The child was just going to run across the road when his mother pulled him back.*

give off emit. *I don't like the smell that paint gives off.*

put off (1) postpone or delay doing something. *You can't put off going to the dentist's forever.* (2) give someone a bad impression of something. *He put me off going to see the play. He said it was awful.*

send off (for) apply to get something through the post. *I'll send off for an application form today.*

pull off succeed. *We've pulled it off at last. We've won first prize.*

put down land (an aeroplane, etc.) *The pilot managed to put down in a nearby field.*

send down expel (from university). *Roger was caught cheating in an exam so was sent down at the end of his first year.* ▶

pull down demolish (a building). *The old theatre was pulled down when the new one was built.*

put over communicate. *You'll need some pictures to help put over your ideas to the audience.*

send over cause something to be delivered by hand (usually to somewhere close by). *A letter for you was delivered to our house. I'll send my husband over with it.*

pull over drive a car to the side of the road and stop it. *Pull over at the next lay-by.*

take on (1) employ. *We're taking on another secretary soon.* (2) do extra work. *Jim's taken on too much.*

drive on keep driving. *Drive on. I don't like stopping for hitch-hikers.*

break up end a marriage or boyfriend/girlfriend relationship. *Henry and Julia have broken up.*

take up start a hobby or start learning a musical instrument. *Susan's taken up the flute.*

drive up *Can you drive that lorry up the hill?*

break in enter a house or flat to steal something. *The thief broke in through the back door.*

take in (1) deceive. *She was taken in by his charm but he isn't really a very nice person.* (2) make clothes smaller. *I've lost weight. I'll have to take this skirt in.*

fall in collapse. *The roof fell in because it was so old.*

drive in *You can drive in and leave the car in front of the house.*

break away leave the main group. *Her supporters broke away to form a new party.*

take away (1) remove something. *Take away those dirty dishes and wash them.* (2) subtract. *Six take away two is four.*

fall away do badly after a good start. *She was good at maths at first but her marks have really fallen away lately.*

drive away *He took the car and drove it away.*

get through (1) succeed (*get through the exam* = pass it). (2) make your way through a crowd or a small space. *He got through a gap in the fence.* (3) do work. *I can't get through all this homework by tomorrow.*

let through clear a space or a path for someone. *Let him through. He's a doctor.*

go through study or read carefully. *I've gone through my essay to check for mistakes three times.*

tear through go very quickly (especially on a motorbike or in a car). *They tore through the estate, frightening everybody.*

get out become known. *The news of his death got out before his family could be told.*

let out (1) release an animal from a room or cage. *I let the dog out for a run in the garden today.* (2) make clothes larger. *I'm getting fat. I'll have to let this skirt out.*

go out have an evening of entertainment outside the house. *We haven't been out for six weeks.*

tear out *Your little boy has just torn a page out of the book I was reading.*

get up get out of bed in the morning. *I get up at six-thirty every morning.*

let up do less. *Don't let up and you're sure to win.* ►

go up be built. *New shopping centres are going up near every large town.*
tear up tear into pieces. *The homework was completely wrong so he tore the piece of paper up into small pieces and started again.*
get about see a lot of people and go to a lot of places. *I get about more now that I'm retired.*
go about do something or start to do something. *How do I go about checking this homework?*
tear about rush around (often used critically). *She tears about trying to help but just gets in the way.*

---

64 Kids!

[page 30]
Person B

Write five statements or opinions about children. Make some of the statements negative and some positive. Add a question tag asking for agreement to each one.
Example: *Children make a lot of noise, don't they?*

A is also writing five statements about children. Agree or disagree with each of A's statements. Example:
A: *Children aren't difficult to look after, are they?*
B: *No, they're not.* (OR *Yes, they are.*)

Listen and reply to A's statements. Then say your five statements to A. Stop after each statement to give A time to speak. A starts this activity.

---

65 Matching them up

[page 124]

a (iv) b (i) c (iii) d (ii)

---

66 World records

[page 66]

a The tallest man in the world
b The biggest weight gain in the world
c The most children ever born to one mother
d The most sets of teeth grown by one person
e The smallest amount of sunshine in the world (at the South Pole)
f The country in which most different languages are spoken
g The world's best selling single (record)
h The world's smallest television (a wristwatch TV)
i The highest number of murders in one city
j The world's largest television audience (for *Live Aid* in July 1985)

67 Drugs kill

[page 122]

MR ROPER I didn't say she should never leave the house at all. I just said she shouldn't go to that café and she shouldn't see that boy any more, that's all.

MRS ROPER All I could think of when Sheena told me that she took drugs was that she was going to die. I let her know at the time, she could go to that café in the afternoon if she wanted to but, as I told her, the evening is for homework. I said please don't go to places like that café.

SHEENA I was not on drugs and when Dad accused me of taking them I was so angry. I was going to say I wasn't on drugs and never had been, but I never got the chance. And then he said I couldn't go out. Just like that. And as for Gary, he told Mum and Dad that my boyfriend sold drugs and that I was wasting my life instead of doing my schoolwork. He's always been jealous of me.

GARY I saved Sheena's life and that's all I care about. That boyfriend of hers was found dead from drugs a year later. He was twenty. I said at the time, drugs can kill you. I explained to her that she ought to be studying because she is the clever one. Dad, of course, tried to stop her going out at all, which was silly. And Mum said she could only go out in the afternoon which was even sillier. Anyway, it worked out OK in the end. Sheena is at university now, having a good time. And she keeps away from pushers.

68 Sorting them out

[page 92]

1 *beautiful* (adjective), *table* (noun), *sat* (verb)

2 **Manner:** *nastily, fast*
Time: *yet, recently, eventually*
Place: *anywhere, upstairs*

69 After the party

[page 16]
Person B

It is after the party. All the furniture and the other things that you discussed with A in part 1 of the activity have been moved. Say where they all are now and ask A for an explanation of how they came to be there. Use the drawing of the living room if you want to.
Example: *This sofa was along the wall in the corner of the room. Why is it now in the middle of the room?*

Start the activity as soon as you are both ready. Either of you can start.

70 Windows

[page 10]
Person B

1 Listen to your partner's description of two pictures and try to remember exactly what A says about them. Take notes if you need to.

2 Describe these pictures to A. You can describe the pictures as many times as A wants you to.

71 Caroline: Part 1

[page 130]

Answer key

Unit 1

1
1. Please be quiet. I'm trying to read the paper.
2. This is a very quiet town. Where do people go in the evenings?
3. I'm working in a factory until I can find a better job.
4. What are you doing with all that paper and glue?
5. I'm not using the computer at the moment so you can use it.
6. Do Karen and John ever write to you?

2
1. remembers
2. smell
3. knows
4. don't hate, don't like
5. Do you know

3
1. Yes, it **does** rain here in the summer.
2. Yes, they **do** get up before eleven o'clock.
3. No, he **doesn't** live near Helen.
4. No, it **isn't** over there.
5. Yes, he **is** the right person for the job.

4
1. are you doing
2. I'm learning
3. I'm working
4. Do you like
5. are giving
6. work (Also possible: am working)
7. tells
8. work
9. don't get
10. prefer
11. I'm working
12. It's becoming
13. They're asking
14. You're

Unit 2

1
1. Would you like me to
2. I could
3. Would you like me to
4. I could
5. Would you like me to

2
1. Shall/Can I
2. I'll/I can
3. I'll/I can
4. I'll/I can
5. shall I/can I

3
1. can
2. How about
3. Why don't
4. Shall
5. Let's
6. Why don't (*can* is possible but may not be a suggestion)
7. Shall (*can* is possible but may not be a suggestion)
8. How about
9. How about
10. can, can

4
1. Why don't we go to the cinema?
2. How about playing tennis?
3. Could Phil get the tickets for you?
4. Can I/Shall I take those boxes for you?
5. Can I/Shall I help you with the coffee?

Unit 3

1
1. at, at
2. on, in
3. on, in
4. in, in
5. on, at

2
1. in, on
2. into
3. on, on
4. into, onto
5. into, on (Also possible: onto)

3
1 during, at
2 in, in
3 on, at, in
4 for, from . . . to, in
5 at, on
6 at, during
7 in, at

4
1 until
2 by
3 by
4 until
5 by

Unit 4

1
1 Were you using the hairdrier when the lights went out?
2 John was not talking to Barbara. Barbara was not even in the room.
3 The last time I saw him, Dick was drinking orange juice in the kitchen.
4 Were you driving slowly when you saw the man in the road?
5 It was snowing as I left home for the last time.

2
1 The bus was (just) stopping when the child jumped off.
2 Jane was writing the last sentence of her homework when her friend asked her to do his as well.
3 While Anna was having/eating dinner at Harry's she lost her necklace.
4 I was still finishing/eating the chips when John brought the sweet in.
5 Was Emily wearing that dress when she got married?

3
1 As I was eating my dinner, there was a knock on the door.
2 Camilla was just getting into the car, when Henry shouted a warning.
3 While you were dancing at the disco, I was painting/I painted the kitchen at home.
4 I knew her ten years ago, when she was working for Star Electronics at the same time as I was.
5 James heard a noise while he was listening to the music.

4
1 was walking
2 saw
3 noticed
4 had
5 was wearing
6 was carrying
7 was just crossing
8 was not avoiding
9 was
10 went across/was going across
11 followed
12 wondered/was wondering
13 was still thinking
14 turned round
15 looked at/were looking at
16 looked
17 said
18 stared at
19 was
20 was also

Unit 5

1
1 not possible
2 He would meet her every time she came to Madrid.
3 I would go swimming twice a day when we lived on the coast.
4 not possible
5 not possible
6 When she lived at home, Laura would borrow her parents' car to drive into town.
7 We would leave our cat with the neighbours when we went on holiday.

2
1 Did you use to
2 used to
3 didn't use to
4 didn't use to
5 used to
6 used to
7 Did you use to
8 used to

3 1 Last week I went to London.
2 I often used to see Peter when we were in the same football team.
3 Sheila wrote to me for six months.
4 When I was young I had only three smart shirts.
5 He **will** eat with his mouth open, which is very irritating.

4 1 used to be
2 used to/would get up
3 not possible
4 used to/would begin
5 used to/would steal
6 used to/would throw
7 used to be
8 will tell
9 will tell
10 used to/would drive
11 used to/would get into
12 not possible
13 not possible
14 will tell
15 not possible

Unit 6

1 1 Did you go to Paris last year?
2 Where is Tom today?
3 Where does Tom live at the moment? (Also possible: Where is Tom living at the moment?)
4 Has Dean got any money these days?
5 Did your friends drive here today?
6 What is the dialling code for Oxford from London?
7 Which cases are Leo's and who do the others belong to?

2 1 How long does it take to get to London by train?
2 Why are you laughing and who are you laughing at?
3 When did you buy that jacket?
4 Which instruments do you play nowadays?
5 Where are the plates and why don't you keep them in the kitchen?

3 1 Who put that on my desk?
2 Where did James leave his umbrella?
3 Whose luggage is that?
4 Which one does she mean?
5 How far did they have to drive before they got to the camp site?
6 What made all the trains late?

4 1 Could you tell me what qualifications he needs?
2 Can you remember what time John left?
3 Do you know when Sally's coming?
4 I wonder how much it costs to rent a flat here.
5 I was wondering where I can change this money.
6 Have you any idea how long Phil has been living here?
7 Do you think Peter and Jean are going to be late?
8 I'd like to know what time the shops open in the morning.

5 1 wasn't it
2 can he
3 mustn't we
4 isn't she
5 did you
6 aren't you
7 have you

Unit 7

1 1 This is the second time you've been late this week.
2 Have you ever tried Richard's home-made cakes?
3 How many countries have you lived in?
4 I've already told you the answer.
5 I'm surprised that this car has never broken down before.

2 1 took, had
2 ate
3 took, danced
4 stayed, got up, did
5 made, taught

3
1 have never flown
2 flew, took
3 Have you eaten
4 Did you eat, did you only have
5 has left
6 left
7 have lost
8 lost, left

4
1 Did you see
2 have just come
3 has been
4 didn't go
5 has seen
6 sent
7 saw

Unit 8

1
1 must
2 had to
3 has to
4 must
5 have to
6 have got to (Also possible: have to)

2
1 are supposed to
2 ought to
3 am supposed to
4 ought not to
5 are not supposed to, are supposed to
6 ought not to

3
1 Don't/You must not eat fried food.
2 Don't/You must not drive through the town centre too quickly.
3 Don't/You must not get off the bus until I have got the tickets.
4 Don't/You must not touch the cooker.

Unit 9

1
These are WRONG:
1 (c)
2 (c)
3 (a), (b)
4 (b)
5 (a)
6 (a)
7 (a)
8 (a), (b), (c)
9 (a), (c)
10 (a), (c)

2
1 news, is
2 clothes, has
3 scissors, need
4 goods, arrive
5 Politics, does not have to
6 police, spend
7 glasses, are

3
1 nobody (OR no one)
2 anybody (OR anyone)
3 Everybody (OR Everyone)
4 Nothing, anybody (OR anyone)
5 anybody (OR anyone), anything
6 Everything

Unit 10

1
1 (a)
2 (b)
3 (a)
4 (b)
5 (b)
6 (a)

2
1 have remembered
2 have been remembering
3 has preferred
4 has believed
5 has been tasting

3
1 He has not done enough work.
He has not been doing enough work.
2 He has started this new subject well.
3 He has made a bit more effort this term.
He has been making a bit more effort this term.
4 He has not learned to behave properly in class yet.
5 He has never liked maths, and he has done/has been doing very little work all term.

4
1 has been working/has worked
2 has been training/has trained
3 have been watching/have watched
4 has been
5 has been
6 has never attempted
7 has been helping/has helped
8 has learned/has been learning
9 has not been
10 has applied

Unit 11

1
1 Can I borrow your pen?
2 Excuse me, may I ask a question?
3 Could you change a five-pound note for me, please?
4 Can/Could I have the chocolate one with the cream on top?
5 Can/Could I have a biscuit/one?
6 May/Could I go to a higher level class, please?
7 May/Could I have another cup of coffee?
8 May I borrow/read your newspaper? OR Can/Could I have a look at your newspaper, please?

2
1 Can/will you pass me my book, please?
2 Could I have some chicken soup for dinner?/Would you make me some chicken soup for dinner?
3 Would you stop smoking, please?
4 Would/could you stop people bringing me any more fruit?
5 Could/would you get me some magazines to read, please?

3
1 Would
2 may
3 may
4 Would
5 would
6 may
7 Would
8 may
9 May

Unit 12

1
1 (a)
2 (b)
3 (a)
4 (b)
5 (a)

2
1 (b)
2 (b)
3 (a), (a)
4 (b)
5 (b), (b)

3
1 (b)
2 (a)
3 (b)
4 (a)
5 (b)

4
1 any
2 *no article*, a, a lot of, any/a lot of
3 any, a
4 *no article*, Some (Also possible: A lot of)
5 *no article*

5 I went to *the* bank yesterday in order to arrange for *a* cashpoint card and *a* credit card but I was told that I had to make *a* written application. My name is Doris Winter and I am *a* German national, staying in *the* United Kingdom for one year to improve my English. I was also asked to provide details of my bank account in Germany. *The* account is at *a* bank in Hamburg. *The* enclosed cheque has my account number on it. I understand that *the* credit card they provided cannot be used here. You may contact *the* manager (Mr Fuchs) who will provide *a* reference for me if you require one.

Unit 13

1
1 had eaten
2 had died
3 had not beaten
4 had stopped (smoking)
5 had taken

2
1 had been smoking
2 had been stealing
3 had been playing
4 had been visiting
5 had been reading

3
1 went, had left
2 retired, had worked
3 saw, laughed
4 had visited, caught

4
1 had finished
2 had become
3 had won
4 had become
5 had you been playing
6 had been playing
7 had beaten
8 had been winning
9 had not been hitting
10 had damaged

Unit 14

1
1 There was a tall man at the party whose wife could not come because she was ill.
2 There was a journalist there whose work took her to lots of different countries.
3 I met a lot of new people at the party whose names I can't remember.
4 I talked to a woman whose car had broken down on the way to the party.
5 I was introduced to a man whose brother I had seen on television the evening before.

2
1 whose
2 which
3 whose
4 which
5 which

3
1 where
2 who/that
3 whose
4 which/that
5 whose
6 who/that
7 which/that
8 who

4
1 A briefcase belonging to the Managing Director has been found in Room 253.
2 That burglar sentenced to five years in prison is a neighbour of ours.
3 I heard some people shouting in the street./I heard some people in the street shouting.
4 The man hurt in the accident was taken to hospital.
5 The fence broken by the children has been mended.

Unit 15

1
1 more slowly than
2 cheaper than
3 more expensive than, worse
4 more important than
5 faster than
6 later than
7 more often than
8 friendlier than

2
1 as well as Mary.
2 the more you pay in tax.
3 as clever as
4 the happier you will feel about the examination.
5 the less we will have to do later.

3
1 the most interesting
2 the longest
3 the fastest
4 the most beautifully
5 the biggest

4
1 the least
2 the worst
3 further than/farther than
4 earlier than
5 quieter

Unit 16

1
1 came round
2 put . . . off
3 going in for
4 put . . . up
5 get away with
6 took . . . over, makes up for
7 getting up to

2
1 get round to
2 get on with
3 get on with
4 get by
5 get over

3
1 take off
2 made . . . up
3 go ahead
4 gone off
5 put up with
6 took up
7 made . . . up
8 do . . . up/put . . . on

4
1 We can't put them up because we haven't got room.
2 Did you come across Ronald when you were in Washington?
3 Can you do them up, please?
4 Can you do up these buttons, please?/Can you do these buttons up, please?
5 The dustmen took the rubbish away before seven this morning.

Unit 17

1
1 should/had better
2 shouldn't/had better not
3 should/had better
4 had better not/shouldn't
5 shouldn't/had better not

2
1 Should I go to the Indian restaurant or the Chinese one?
2 Should I take the motorbike or go by bus?
3 Should I cook dinner or buy a take-away meal?
4 Should I finish my homework or go out?
5 Should I wear the striped shirt or the pink one?

3
1 He shouldn't have left the chicken in the oven so long.
2 She should have used a sharper saw.
3 He shouldn't have called an ambulance.
4 She should have told her earlier.
5 He should have started working for his exams earlier.

4
1 don't need to, don't have to, needn't
2 need to
3 doesn't need to, doesn't have to, needn't
4 doesn't need to, doesn't have to, needn't
5 don't need to, don't have to, needn't

5
1 Arthur needn't have worried.
2 Beverley needn't have handed it in until the following week.
3 Eric needn't have brought his guitar.
4 Lily needn't have phoned the police.

Unit 18

1
1 I am buying/I am going to buy
2 he is arriving
3 her boyfriend is not coming/is not going to come
4 you are definitely going to pass
5 Are you working/Are you going to work

2
1 shall
2 he'll
3 I'll
4 won't
5 shall

3
1 I'll take it to the post office for you.
2 I won't take the car at all. I'll walk.
3 It's Jane's birthday in August. She'll be sixteen.
4 He is going to meet Mary at the station.
5 It's going to rain.

4
1 is going to buy, am going to cook
2 closes
3 I'll drive
4 won't know/aren't going to know
5 I'm seeing
6 stops (will stop/is going to stop)
7 She's taking

5
1 I'm not going to phone/I won't phone
2 Are you going (Also possible: Are you going to go)
3 I'm not going (Also possible: I'm not going to go)
4 I'll go
5 won't dance
6 I'm not playing/I won't play/I'm not going to play
7 I'll stop
8 is starting/is going to start
9 will be/are going to be
10 I'll phone

Unit 19

1
1 may/might/could be watching
2 may/might not be coming
3 may/might/could be taking
4 Might/Could John be leaving
5 may/might not be playing

2
1 may/might/could have forgotten
2 may/might not have heard (*He couldn't have heard* is also possible, but this would be deduction.)
3 may/might/could have dropped
4 may/might/could have told
5 may/might/could have gone out

3
1 should/ought to have been
2 should/ought to have told
3 should/ought to have won
4 should/ought to have arrived
5 should/ought to have done

4
1 can't/couldn't have been
2 can't/couldn't have been
3 must have got
4 must have passed
5 can't/couldn't have gone

5
1 It could/might have been my parents.
2 . . ., but could/might he have come back later?
3 Look at her. She can't be more than fifteen.
4 You must be Arthur's sister.
5 It's five o'clock now, so he really should/ought to arrive here by seven.

Unit 20

1
1 (e) 4 (a)
2 (b) 5 (d)
3 (c)

2
1 calls back, I'll fax
2 would buy, owned
3 send, they'll arrive, send, they'll get
4 would earn, paid, made
5 phones, will speak
6 asks, won't be
7 have finished/finish, don't sit
8 would use, didn't have

3
1 (Example)
2 If I had learned to do maths at primary school, I would have taken jobs that used numbers.
3 If I had worked harder at secondary school, I would have passed my examinations.
4 If I had learned to dance at the youth club, I wouldn't have been shy with girls.
5 If I had learned to speak clearly at job interviews, I would have done better at them.
6 If I had worked hard at the office, I would have got promotion.

Unit 21

1
1 have . . . out
2 drop in
3 turn . . . down
4 gone down
5 grows up
6 Slow down
7 put . . . out
8 warm up
9 let . . . in
10 plugged . . . in

2
1 call . . . off/put . . . off
2 drop . . . off
3 shave . . . off
4 rang off

3
1 runs out
2 put off
3 send it off
4 dash/rush off
5 get off
6 pop out
7 sold/run out of
8 calm down
9 given up

Unit 22

1
1 already
2 still
3 yet
4 soon
5 lately
6 late

2
1 during
2 throughout
3 during
4 for
5 Since

3
1 in the fridge
2 on the top shelf
3 on the corner
4 on the left
5 outside the door

4
1 excitedly
2 deliberately
3 carelessly
4 miserably
5 quietly
6 honestly
7 happily

Unit 23

1
1 not possible
2 Eighty per cent of what we produce is exported.
3 not possible
4 Trainee pilots are expected to land an aircraft after twenty hours of instruction.
5 The papers will be sent to you immediately.
6 not possible
7 Your bill is just being added up.
8 not possible
9 By the time I arrived all your letters had already been opened.

2
1 We were promised our money back.
2 They were told that the hotel was near the sea.
3 Harriet was always being called stupid.
4 The last tickets had been sold (just before we got to the box office).
5 She should have been stopped.

3
1 If you are required for an interview, you will be notified by letter tomorrow.
2 His trousers were held up by a safety pin which was pinned to his shirt.
3 Parcels cannot be sent through the post tied up with string.
4 The car was (being) hit by falling rocks as we drove along the valley.
5 The roof of this church has just been repaired with local wood.

4
1 are wanted
2 was held up
3 was threatened
4 was being stolen
5 was tied up
6 were also stolen
7 was not taken
8 has/had been used OR was used

5
1 is sent
2 is diluted
3 are added
4 have been added
5 is mixed
6 (is) heated
7 be heated
8 be added

Unit 24

1
1 (Example)
2 She will be having breakfast with the architect and (will be) discussing the new building at eight-thirty.
3 She will be telephoning Tom in New York to wish him a Happy Birthday at nine-fifteen.
4 She will be dictating letters at nine-thirty.
5 She will be having a meeting with J and M about the Compact order at ten o'clock.
6 She will be talking to the new trainees at eleven o'clock.
7 She will be writing a report of the J and M meeting at eleven-thirty.
8 She will be having lunch with the new Sales Manager at twelve-thirty.

2
1 Will you be using the computer later today?
2 Will you be doing the washing up next week?
3 Will you be needing the car this evening?

3
1 will have done
2 will have started
3 Will . . . have built . . .
4 will have danced
5 won't have turned off, won't have thought

4
1 will have learned
2 will have discovered
3 won't have found
4 will we have contacted
5 will we have learned

Unit 25

1
1 We could go to Scotland for our holiday this year.
2 I'd rather not go out this evening.
3 Please remember to feed the cat twice a day.
4 I remember paying for these tins at the checkout.
5 Don't risk playing tennis before your arm gets better.

2
1 going out
2 coming back
3 to go on
4 to find
5 doing

3
1 to write
2 to see
3 speaking
4 writing
5 to do
6 to be
7 changing
8 making
9 doing
10 cleaning
11 to find

4
1 making
2 to turn down
3 to accept
4 to call
5 to disturb
6 to invite
7 to come
8 saying

Unit 26

1
1 completely
2 extremely
3 complete
4 extremely
5 complete
6 extremely
7 complete, extremely
8 extremely, completely

2
1 enormous
2 absolute
3 extremely
4 really
5 quite
6 quite
7 really
8 extremely
9 absolutely
10 total
11 fairly
12 quite

3
1 absolutely (Also possible: extremely)
2 extremely
3 enormous
4 slightly
5 real

Unit 27

1
1 for
2 to
3 about
4 about
5 about
6 from
7 for
8 for

2
1 about/at
2 of
3 with
4 at/by
5 of

3
1 of
2 to
3 between (not *with* as both nouns follow the preposition. *Does your holiday have any connection with this book?* is possible.)
4 to
5 for

4
1 for
2 in
3 with
4 of
5 of
6 at
7 to
8 for

Unit 28

1
1 to see
2 working
3 to be
4 losing
5 to see
6 to share

2
1 Henry's girlfriend persuaded him to see a doctor yesterday.
2 Richard's friends made him see that horror film, even though he didn't want to.
3 Juliette's parents didn't let her stay up later than ten o'clock when she was twelve.
4 I was listening to the birds singing when you came in this morning.
5 I saw Mr Wilson painting his house last week. That was before his accident forced him to leave it half-painted.

3
1 write
2 leaving
3 not to accept
4 to offer
5 to go on

4
1 to confirm
2 to bring
3 improving
4 to use
5 to bring
6 handing in
7 registering
8 to meet

Unit 29

1
1. Trevor said (that) he went/had gone to a concert with Mary.
2. Dad explained that he didn't do/hadn't done any housework.
3. Tracy said (that) Harry did not/doesn't want to dance.
4. He told us he is/was paying for the bread.
5. She said she has/had finished.

2
1. Mr Williams asked John if he had found the hammer.
2. Ms Fowler asked Dave if he was from Edinburgh.
3. Jenny asked Jean if she knew what 'versatile' meant.
4. Lynn asked Tessa if she would go out with David again.
5. Peter asked Susan if she was playing tennis on Friday.

3
1. She told Peter to remember his keys.
2. The Managing Director told everybody to expect a good profit.
3. The teacher told Kate to do some extra homework.
4. Henry asked Gemma to marry him three times last year.

4
1. Brian explained that Henry should press the red button.
2. Mary told Lesley to see a doctor.
3. Tim thought that more people ought to use recycled paper.
4. James hoped that it would snow this winter.
5. Richard suggested that we went out for a meal.
6. Gemma said that she had had a good day at work.

Unit 30

1
1. Sometimes I go . . ./I sometimes go . . ./. . . on my own sometimes.
2. . . . hardly finished eating . . . (Also possible: Hardly had we finished . . .)
3. She really ought not to . . ./Really she ought not to . . ./. . . all the time really.
4. Do you ever want . . .
5. I will never know . . .
6. She often takes . . .
7. She is often . . .

2
1. I always forget . . .
2. Correct (Also possible: . . . answered my letter yet.)
3. . . . on the phone since four o'clock.
4. Correct
5. . . . dances quite well actually.
6. Possible (BUT You really must . . . is more natural.)
7. He has been very depressed lately.
8. On Thursday I will . . ./. . . information on Thursday.
9. Anyway, we can't . . ./We can't go yet anyway . . .
10. Of course, she isn't ready . . ./She isn't, of course, ready . . .

3
1. There's a brown file in the desk drawer./In the desk drawer there's a brown file.
2. I'll see you here on Monday.
3. She always criticizes your work in a very polite way.
4. A few weeks ago I ordered a new computer./I ordered a new computer a few weeks ago.
5. Please put that down carefully over there before you go.

4
1. often
2. around
3. never
4. far
5. there
6. unhappily
7. everywhere
8. back
9. cheerfully

Unit 31

1
1. Linda seems bored and fed up.
2. Vicky isn't very good at Spanish. She isn't good at French either.
3. Brenda often helps Paul with the washing up. She also repairs the car . . .
4. Neither Bob nor his father like fish. They . . .
5. The Andersons aren't coming and Jean and John Dixon aren't either.
6. You can use the computer at either three o'clock or five o'clock but not at both times.
7. We can tell Matthew the bad news now or later.

2
1. but
2. although
3. unless

3
1. We have no money **so** we can't buy your mother a present.
2. The football match was cancelled **because of** the rain.
3. Jim told Sally he didn't want to see her any more **because** he had met another girl.
4. Camels manage well in the desert **because** they can go a long time without water.

4
1. . . ., but I'll speak to you as soon as I've finished talking to this lady. (Also possible: . . . when I've finished . . .)
2. Diane caught the vase just as it fell off the shelf. (Also possible: . . . when it fell . . .)
3. I can be chopping the meat while you are getting the vegetables ready.
4. Claire and Jason were happily married when I saw them last.
5. Please tell Joanna to come half an hour earlier than usual, when you see her next week.

Unit 32

1
1. the car door OR the door of the car
2. Saturday's football match
3. a loaf of bread
4. in the corner of the room
5. the coffee cups
6. a glass of orange juice

2
1. I have been a Beatles fan since I was twelve.
2. She has never liked rock music.
3. Have you ever gone/been to a late-night cinema show?
4. We don't see her much these days.
5. Do you have any serious health problems at the moment?

3
1. it's
2. There is/There's
3. It was
4. There was
5. There are, it will be

4
1. We are having a really great time here at the moment.
2. The weather has been brilliant, though there were some clouds in the sky today.
3. The hotel is not too bad, but there are too many tourists and the staff are getting fed up.
4. The food, however, is exceptionally good.
5. Tomorrow we hope to go on a trip organized by the hotel and see some of the local sights.